PIONEER MISSIONARY, EVANGELICAL STATESMAN

A Life of A T (Tim) Houghton

Timothy Yates

authorHOUSE®

AuthorHouse™ UK Ltd.
500 Avebury Boulevard
Central Milton Keynes, MK9 2BE
www.authorhouse.co.uk
Phone: 08001974150

First published by AuthorHouse   04/15/2011

ISBN: 978-1-4567-7231-4 (sc)
ISBN: 978-1-4567-7233-8 (hc)
IESB: 978-1-4567-7230-7 (e)

DEDICATION

This book is dedicated by his sisters and brother to Pat Houghton, elder son of Canon and Mrs Houghton, who died on 8th June 2010 shortly before the manuscript was completed. He had been delighted to know that publication of his father's biography was in hand. Pat was always proud to have been the first baby born to serving BCMS missionaries.

CONTENTS

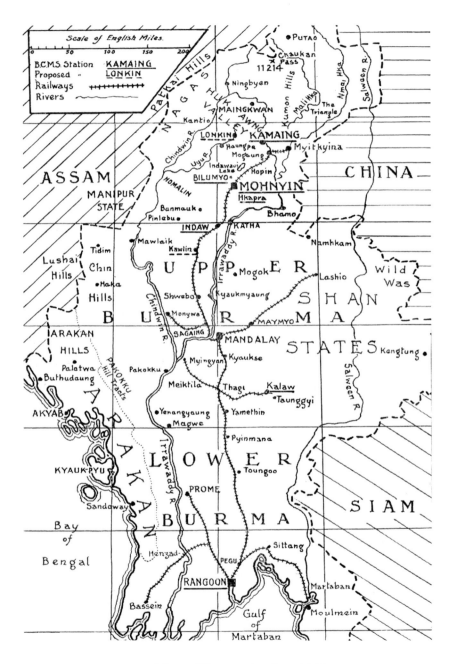

Map of Burma in the 1930's

FOREWORD
By John B Taylor, former Bishop of St Albans

To me he has always been Canon Houghton, a missionary statesman and a man of great stature. With a person of my father's generation and of his worldwide experience it would just not have been right for me to descend to the cosiness of Christian name terms. I respected him too much for that. His name was coterminous with evangelical missionary strategy and he was the personification of the Bible Churchman's Missionary Society. That is how I knew him. My only concern was how to distinguish him from his equally famous brother, Bishop Frank Houghton of the China Inland Mission. Later on I met them together and he was laughingly telling me how he too would have been a bishop had not his kit gone to the bottom of the ocean thanks to enemy action while he was on his way to be consecrated Bishop of Mandalay. But both brothers were clearly Episcopal, whatever their orders may have been.

I first heard him speak at the Nottingham Faith and Order Conference of the British Council of Churches in 1964. It was the year when the ecumenical movement made real efforts to involve representatives of the growing evangelical movement. Perhaps that was why I was there. It was certainly why he was a platform speaker. He was clear in his speech, theological in his content and masterly in his presentation. He was listened to with respect. My regard for him grew by the minute.

A few weeks later as a member of staff at Oak Hill College, I attended church with my family at Christ Church Cockfosters and found to my surprise and delight that in the row in front of us in the south transept was none other than Canon Houghton with his wife Coralie, their daughter Elizabeth (Betty) Simmons with Peter and their lovely young children. We used to see them most Sundays and it was lovely to get to know them. Then one Sunday Canon Houghton was due to preach on his home turf – something to look forward to.

During prayers before the sermon, the Vicar, Kenneth Hooker, called for the prayers of the congregation for the Simmons family. Their youngest child, Jonathan, had been taken ill in the night and despite frantic efforts to perform a tracheotomy on the kitchen table to enable him to breathe, he had died. The congregation was devastated. So were we. But what would the preacher preach? As he climbed into the pulpit we marvelled that he was still going to speak out the message that the Lord had laid on his heart for the people. How, I wondered, could any man have the courage to face a congregation the morning after losing a beloved grandchild? We felt we were listening to the voice of a saint.

Years later I enjoyed the privilege of speaking occasionally at the Keswick Convention under his benign chairmanship. For a new boy like me, he was invariably supportive and encouraging. My nervousness evaporated and slowly confidence grew. For that I shall always be grateful.

Then came the moment of highest privilege, to be invited to attend the sixtieth anniversary of his ordination on December 19th 1981 in Christ Church Barnet, where he was now living, and to give the blessing. But I was by then the new Bishop of St Albans and Christ Church was outside of my jurisdiction — by about a mile! What would the Bishop of London think? But John Stott was preaching and Canon Houghton had invited me, so I pretended it was my day off and duly showed up to join in the celebrations for a remarkable, and still unfinished, ministry.

Soli Deo Gloria

AUTHOR'S PREFACE

I must express my gratitude to the family of Canon Houghton for entrusting his biography to me. Special thanks must go to two of his sons-in-law and their wives: Canon Campbell Matthews and Mrs Monica Matthews, who first approached me on the project; and Prebendary Peter Pytches and Mrs Beryl Pytches, who have helped me with timely loans and promptings during the extended process. I must also express appreciation to the extended family who have shown great patience when progress must have seemed slow. I must also express here my indebtedness to Lynne Firth whose secretarial help and support have been invaluable.

This is the place to explain certain aspects of the text. Canon Houghton left some two thousand handwritten pages of autobiography, which covered his life from 1896-1958 and the period following his retirement from BCMS (now Crosslinks) from 1966-1975. Although he never fully completed this account, the existence of daily desk diaries from 1940-1984 has meant that there is a further full documentary source. In the text, where there is a quotation without any ascription, the words will be taken from the relevant section of the autobiography. After 1940, I have included dates in brackets which refer not necessarily to the date of the event, but to the date it was recorded in the diary. Further researchers who want to know about developments in conservative evangelicalism from 1940 will find these diaries an essential source. Earlier diaries for the period in Burma (1924-1939) fell victim to the invasion of Burma by the Japanese: but the autobiography does rest on contemporary sources, as Canon Houghton still possessed his letters to supporters of those days to prompt his memory when recording the story in his eighties. It is intended eventually that the original manuscripts will be laid up in the archive of the University of Birmingham, where all the original papers of the CMS are also to be found.

It was a matter of great regret that Patrick Houghton, Canon Houghton's eldest son, died while this book was being completed. He did read much of the manuscript and his memory of the incident when the family were bombed in Bristol in 1940 has been included. The family lived through stirring times and Canon Houghton's life was one of some drama, subject like St Paul to shipwreck and some dangers on the mission field, followed by much labour at home for the missionary society and many other Christian bodies and causes. It is to be hoped that his level of commitment and service may be an inspiration to others who confront the challenges of a new century for Christian discipleship.

Timothy Yates.

ACKNOWLEDGEMENTS

First and foremost the Houghton family wishes to express profound gratitude to Canon Timothy Yates for his willingness to undertake the task of writing this biography. In his preface he himself alludes to the extensive autobiographical material which formed the basis of this work. We are most appreciative of his thorough research and his apt portrayal of a life at home and in ministry.

The family wishes to express special thanks to the Revd. John Stott for his permission to include his address at Canon Houghton's funeral service, also to Nigel Holmes, formerly of Radio Cumbria, for suggesting the inclusion of material from a BBC radio interview with Canon Houghton and to the BBC Archives Dept. for permission to do so.

Appreciation is also expressed to Bishop John Taylor, formerly Bishop of St Albans, and Professor John Wolffe, Professor of Religious History at the Open University, for kindly contributing to this volume.

Finally thanks are due to Crosslinks (formerly BCMS) for permission to include photographs from early BCMS publications and to the Church Book Room Press for an address from the Islington Clerical Conference 1947.

ACCESS TO FAMILY DOCUMENTS

It is the family's intention that the autobiographical documents which formed the basis of this study shall eventually be deposited at the library of the University of Birmingham where other Evangelical archives are housed. This will probably be around 2020. In the meantime, where serious academic research is being undertaken, limited access may be made available on enquiry to Preb. Peter Pytches (email: peterpytches@ googlemail.com)

LIST OF ABBREVIATIONS

ABM	American Baptist Mission
ADC	Aide-de-camp
BCMS	Bible Churchmen's Missionary Society
CBMS	Conference of British Missionary Societies
CEEC	Church of England Evangelical Council
CEN	Church of England Newspaper
CICCU	Cambridge Inter-Collegiate Christian Union
CIM	China Inland Mission
CIPBC	Church of India, Pakistan, Burma and Ceylon
CMS	Church Missionary Society
CPAS	Church Pastoral Aid Society
CSI	Church of South India
CSSM	Children's Special Service Mission
DICCU	Durham Inter-Collegiate Christian Union
EFAC	Evangelical Fellowship in the Anglican Communion
GOC	General Officer Commanding
IMC	International Missionary Council
IVF	Inter Varsity Fellowship
LIFCU	London Inter-Faculty Christian Union
MECCA	Missionary & Ecumenical Council of the Church Assembly
MMS	Methodist Missionary Society
MRA	Moral Re-Armament
MSM	Missionary School of Medicine
NEAC	National Evangelical Anglican Congress
OICCU	Oxford Inter-Collegiate Christian Union
RSM	Regimental Sergeant Major
SAMS	South American Missionary Society
SCM	Student Christian Movement
SLI	Somerset Light Infantry
SPCK	Society for Promoting Christian Knowledge
SPG	Society for the Propagation of the Gospel
UCCF	Universities & Colleges Christian Fellowship
WCC	World Council of Churches
YMCA	Young Men's Christian Association

CHAPTER 1

EARLY LIFE 1896 – 1917

Alfred Thomas Houghton was born on the 11th of April 1896. His father, Thomas Houghton, had entered the ordained ministry of the Church of England from a far from easy background. Although Alfred never knew his grandfather on the Houghton side, he knew that he had been a non-commissioned officer in the Army and at some stage had been stationed in Cork, where he had met an Irish girl and formed a mixed Protestant-Roman Catholic marriage in 1853. Alfred judged that his father's reluctance to speak about his family background disguised his own father's problems with alcohol and his mother's Roman Catholicism and explained the two 'most prominent phobias' in Thomas Houghton's life, 'the Church of Rome and drink'.

The family had settled in Manchester after Army life. Thomas Houghton seems to have found personal faith and a call to the ordained ministry through the congregation of St Jude's, Openshaw. Here he was a Sunday School teacher and here he met another teacher in Elizabeth Ann Mosley, who came from Dukingfield in Cheshire. They married on April 6th, 1886. Thomas became a Scripture Reader in the parish with enhanced responsibility and status and studied the Greek New Testament with help from the incumbent, a Mr Watson. He was ordained and became curate in Bolton, at a church which was then held to be an 'Evangelical stronghold'. His marriage was to last 58 years until his wife's death aged 73, judged by her son to be a 'perfect partner', a lover of poetry, intensely feminine, remembered for her peals of laughter at their childhood clowning.

Thomas Houghton was a convinced Protestant, a supporter of the Lord's Day Observance Society and a Calvinist in theology. His son described him in middle years in Sunday dress: he wore a frock coat, top hat and black boots, he had a beard and when in church he preached always in a black gown, which necessitated removing his surplice in the hymn before the sermon. He never wore a cassock. Although the possessor of a musical voice, even classical music was deemed to be 'worldly'. There was singing in church but Sankey's hymns were not approved and there were no anthems or solos. His son judged that he lacked any 'aesthetic or artistic sense'. Flowers or decorations, even at Harvest Festival, were prohibited as leading to 'sensuous worship' and no cross was permitted on the communion table. At home Shakespeare and some poetry was acceptable but the novels of such writers as Walter Scott or Charles Dickens were not. This was not uncommon among the evangelical households of the age: the sons of Henry Venn of CMS remembered that novels were disapproved of in their vicarage home in Drypool, Hull in the 1830's, as was the theatre. This was also true of Thomas Houghton, whose disapproval of the stage extended to forbidding his sons to take part in school plays, a source of disappointment to them.

After curacies in Bolton, (where his vicar died of a heart attack), St Mark's Barrow in Furness (where congregations were very large but the vicar was made archdeacon of Liverpool, Madden by name), Christ Church, Chadderton and St Thomas' Stafford (where it seems the then Lord Lichfield recruited him to assist a vicar suffering from developing paralysis), Thomas Houghton did a final year curacy at Holy Trinity, Derby before being offered the living of Kensington Chapel in Bath, a proprietary chapel in the gift of the Church Patronage Society in December 1898. Here a 'conventional district' had been carved out of the parish of St Saviour's, giving the chapel a population of some 2,000 to serve. By then Thomas and Elizabeth Houghton had a family of six children, Elsie Agnes, known as Agnes (b. 1 January 1887), Herbert (b. 27 May 1890), Eileen May whose second name was chosen because she shared a birthday with George V's Queen Mary (May) of Teck (b. 26 May 1892), Frank, who was to serve with CIM and become a bishop in China (b. 24 April 1894) and Alfred (b. 11 April 1896). Lydia had been born in the year of the move (b. 29 August 1898) and two more children were to follow, Stanley (b. 26 July 1900) and Freda Grace (b. 28 December 1902): Lydia was to become a medical doctor and Stanley, like his two brothers and two sisters (Eileen and Freda), became a missionary. As the living only carried a stipend of £200, and even this dependent on the giving of the chapel's congregation, finance was tight and the home happy but frugal. Alfred remembers living-in maids, usually only one at a time, a three storeyed house with a reasonably spacious garden for children's games and family holidays financed by the generosity of Miss Watney, a well-off friend and committed Christian from the past, who also endeared herself to the family by annually supplying Christmas presents from expensive London stores for every child. Thomas Houghton was to stay in Bath until 1917, a time when Alfred joined the Army, before moving to a Norfolk parish, Whitington, where he stayed until 1949, retiring aged 90 in that year.

Alfred found his upbringing strict but a source of gratitude later. There was occasional physical punishment with a slipper or exile to his room but no parental anger. Despite shortage of income, his parents tithed what they had. No debt was permitted, even if tradesmen would have gladly given credit for goods. This could mean that at times food was scarce and Alfred remembered one week in which the family ate nothing but dried bread: 'I do not think Father would have told anyone else but God about our need, even if we were starving'. There was no pocket money for the children. His father had a rooted objection to State schools (and even to allowing his children to mix with the children of the church's Sunday School) but a generous headmaster retained Herbert at a privately run school after funds ran out and proceeded to give a free education to Frank, Alfred and Stanley at the privately run Victoria College, while the girls were educated by their mother who had taught professionally in earlier life.

Frank was a highly intelligent child and in some measure Alfred felt under his shadow in childhood, dependent for instance upon him when Virgil had to be construed with a visiting clergyman acting as tutor. Their father forbade soccer but cricket was permitted: Alfred enjoyed fielding and one particularly brilliant stop of a fierce drive so impressed the batsman, a certain boy called Pulman, that when they met later in Burma in 1917 he remembered it and as adjutant recommended Alfred for officer cadet training from the Somerset Light Infantry battalion in which both were serving. On the whole Alfred disliked school, though he excelled at Art, to the point of an art master enquiring if he might make a career of it.

Because the family were isolated from other children (something which Alfred regretted in retrospect) they became a self-contained and lively community of their own. Frank and Alfred produced a home-grown family newspaper, Home News, with Frank as editor and Alfred as art editor. One report by the editor of a 'prize-giving' on 17 April 1907, resulting from Agnes' teaching of them in a home Sunday School, recorded 'the marks were all very near...although there was a sharp drop in the case of Mr Alfred Houghton, who was at the bottom. Miss Freda Houghton, we are sorry to say, clapped for herself, and Mr Alfred Houghton who also clapped for himself' – Freda was excused as only aged 4½, it seems. Christmas was always a 'rapturous and mysterious festival' with presents, stockings, crackers and games like blind-man's buff and a favourite of Alfred's called 'Family Coach'. The children sang carols to their parents on Christmas morning. There were musical evenings with a family friend called Miss Cowan playing the piano and Alfred dated his love of music from these evenings. It is a portrait of a fundamentally happy Victorian household with fun and humour as well as discipline and religion. Alfred remembered vividly the Queen's death in 1901, even though only 5½: to him it seemed 'as though the world as I knew it has come to an end... Queen Victoria seemed to symbolise the whole of life as we knew it'.

In recalling his boyhood, Alfred wrote that 'as long as I can remember my greatest ambition was to be a soldier'. In the 'Home News', he did a series of illustrations which aimed to show what each member of the family would one day become: Frank, all too presciently, was to be a bishop but his picture of himself was as a field-marshal. He remembered the boxes of toy soldiers which could be bought in Bath at a shop called 'Commons', situated opposite the Guildhall: each box held six or more lead soldiers of different regiments under a red lid. When the Boer War intervened after 1899, khaki predominated over the uniforms. The family were encouraged to produce 'Birthday Lists' of their most wanted presents: for Alfred, boxes of soldiers were always top of the list. His father tried to dampen his enthusiasm for Army life by reminding him of Spion Kop, where the Boers had pinned down British troops in an exposed position by accurate rifle fire and there had been many casualties: how would he like to lie wounded on Spion Kop with no water in a burning sun? To which he replied that he would not mind: 'all I could think about was military glory'. He was a boy who knew all the British generals by name though only three years old at the outbreak of war: Sir Redvers Buller, Lord Methuen, Baden Powell and Lord Roberts, hero of the relief of Mafeking, were all familiar to him. When Lord Roberts visited Bath his father indulged his love of the military by holding him high on his shoulders to see the great man passing by. If his father suggested that it would be hard to live as a Christian in the army, Alfred would reply that Christians were needed in the Army as everywhere else. General Gordon was his hero and he probably reminded his father of the Christian general who died at Khartoum so heroically. It was to be a bitter blow to Alfred, given the opportunity to enlist as a volunteer in 1915 as an adolescent patriot aged 19, who quoted 'dulce et decorum pro patria mori', that his father would not permit it. The situation was resolved, however, when first Herbert and then Alfred himself were conscripted in 1916 but not before Alfred had experienced some personal 'misery' as a non-combatant owing to his father's refusal. His patriotism also extended to make him fiercely sympathetic of those who resisted Home Rule in Northern Ireland in 1914, whether Sir Herbert Carson or the officers of the Curragh or all who adopted the slogan 'Ulster will fight and Ulster will be right': 'I was strongly in favour of the Ulstermen who were determined not to be handed over'.

Military minded as he may have been, with a mind fixed on army service, Alfred also had another strand running through his life, even in early teen-age. In April 1910, Agnes persuaded him to accompany her to a meeting of CMS at the Guildhall in Bath. Although he agreed to go he was reluctant, not least because he feared an emotional appeal. The speaker was a Canon Heywood, then working in Bombay and later bishop of Mombasa. Alfred could not recall the address, which made little impact and he was preparing to leave with some relief (no emotional appeal had been made), when an elderly lady tapped him on the shoulder from behind and asked 'are you going to be a missionary?' He wrote: 'it was certainly the last thing I wanted to be, at the age of fourteen, and the last thing I wanted to be asked'. Nevertheless 'in my boyish way I somehow sensed that beyond this old lady's embarrassing question was God Himself speaking to me. What could I answer? It seemed an eternity before I heard myself answering "I hope so", and then I knew that I was answering God, and that there was no other answer I could give'.

This proved to be something of a personal marker for Alfred. The children had formed a 'Church Association', to which, aged 14½ he read a paper. His older brother, Herbert, also spoke at this family meeting and concluded by thanking Alfred for his contribution, adding 'another gentleman whose great aspiration, I believe, is to become missionary Archbishop of Antananarivo (Madagascar), or Rural Dean of Timbuctoo, or Archdeacon of Abeokuta (Nigeria) or something of the kind'. The butt of these remarks wrote of them that they 'referred to the crisis in my life which had taken place the year before' that is, at the missionary meeting: otherwise it would have been far nearer the mark to make reference to his ambition to be a Field-Marshal.

Alfred was confirmed at St Peter's, Bath in March 1911. His father was recuperating at Weston-Super-Mare from what his son described as a nervous breakdown but he still wrote a letter of 17 March 1911: 'My dear Alfred, You fully realise that at confirmation a candidate makes a public profession of faith in the Lord Jesus Christ, don't you? The words 'I do' mean a great deal. They mean "I do renounce the world, the flesh and the devil; I do believe in Christ as my Saviour; I do intend God helping me to walk in God's holy will and commandments all the days of my life". I trust you are fully prepared to say those words from your heart as the honest and sincere expression of your thoughts. Write and tell me if this is so, and if you are truly looking to the merits of our Lord Jesus Christ as the sole ground of your salvation. Mother and I fully hope and believe that this is so and we pray that God may grant you special grace, guidance and teaching at this time. With warm love to you and earnest prayer for you at this time, Your affectionate father, Thomas Houghton'. Alfred wrote 'I have treasured this letter all these years and felt thankful that Father led me to think things out for myself and enabled me to answer in the affirmative'. Long afterwards, going through his father's papers, he found his own reply, marked by his father 'Alfred's letter about confirmation March 24/11'. He had written on 19 March 1911: 'Dear Father, I am so glad to be able to say that I can say those words from heart, that I renounce the world, the flesh and the devil; that I believe in Jesus Christ as my Saviour, and with God's help I mean to walk in His holy will and commandments all the days of my life. I know that I am saved, because Jesus Christ has died for me, a sinner, on the cross, and I am looking to His merits as the ground of my salvation. What I should do without being able to turn to him in all my troubles I do not know, except that I know life would not be worth living.

It helps me to think of the life hereafter, when we shall have no troubles or wants. I do not know when I began to look to Jesus and to believe on Him as my Saviour, for it is the same with me, as you said it was with many of the Lord's people, who cannot point to any direct time, when they turned to Him. It is so nice to be able to have someone to help you, wherever you are and in whatever you need; for He has helped me, and always will, in my work at school or anywhere else. If I had not a message that I am longing to take to the heathen, I should not have any desire to be a missionary, but I hope that in a few years I may be able to carry the glad tidings to the poor heathen. Thanking you for your beautiful letter, I remain your loving son, Alfred.'

The experience of confirmation was followed by a nearly fatal accident. The family were on a seaside holiday at Boscombe. Earlier in the day a film unit had been on the beach and caused a mild sensation. Alfred and Frank decided to go from sandbank to sandbank, unaware of the danger of a swift in-coming tide. Swimming back they were still out of their depth, both in difficulties about fifty to a hundred yards out from the shore. Their sister Eileen saw their plight and heard their cries for help. She rushed into the sea fully clothed. A by-stander, who turned out to be a private detective, assumed that this was a staged suicide before realising it was a genuine emergency. He rescued Eileen and dived for Alfred pulling him up by his hair from where he had sunk. At first it was thought that Alfred was alone, until their sister Agnes, desperately fearful for Frank, persuaded the men to swim out for him. Frank needed twenty minutes of artificial respiration to bring him round and, as Alfred noted, it was a miracle that both were saved. Alfred suffered little in after effects but Frank lost half a term through severe congestion of the lungs at Clarence School, Weston-Super-Mare (which later became Canford). Alfred's daily Bible reading from Daily Light for that day included a section of Psalm 40, including 'he brought me up ...out of the horrible pit, out of the miry clay', a passage which thereafter for ever reminded him of this experience, with the phrase which came to his mind again and again 'saved to serve'. Both boys, lying exhausted on their beds in the evening, felt a sense of purpose in the experience of deliverance.

During his father's recuperation from breakdown in Weston-Super-Mare he had been befriended by a headmaster and member of the local Plymouth Brethren assembly by the name of Bill Franklin. Their outlook on many things and on the Christian faith were much in accord and there was mutual respect. This resulted in Franklin offering free education for Frank at his 'Clarence School', on the understanding that Frank would help out with the younger boys in the preparatory school department. Mr Franklin's nephew, J S Macnutt, became vice-principal but he was an ordained Anglican: this resulted in two crocodiles of boys, one moving towards the Plymouth Brethren assembly and one to Holy Trinity church every Sunday. Frank did well and became Head Prefect before moving on to St John's, Highbury on a Peache scholarship to train for the ministry of the Church of England. In 1913 Alfred followed both in the free education and in the care of younger boys but he found the latter taxing: it was his first taste of responsibility but Frank's was a hard act to follow, as a universally popular senior boy. Alfred played in the school soccer XI (his father's earlier prohibitions notwithstanding), enjoyed hockey and athletics, especially sprinting and long jump, and played occasionally for the cricket XI, becoming captain of the second XI. Academically, he had difficulties with the London Inter BA exams, failing in Mathematics at the first attempt. He remembered sitting the exam in London in a building opposite Westminster School in Vincent Square and re-sat successfully in 1915. Like Frank, he had become Head Prefect and felt that, in this capacity, he had been able to make a stand against swearing and card playing in the 'Caput', a group of senior boys. The debate over volunteering for military service took place in this period. Following his father's refusal, he was invited to join the school staff for a short time before conscription in 1916 resolved his unhappiness.

CHAPTER 2

ARMY LIFE AND BURMA

Anthony Eden, who like Alfred joined the Light Infantry, called his memoir of the period 1897-1914 *Another World*. There is no doubt that the Great War marked a watershed between the comparative serenity of the late Victorians and Edwardians and the modern world. For Alfred Houghton it was the break between a protected, religious childhood and the rougher world of barrack-room life and Army discipline. It was, however, a life for which he had longed as a child; as a young man, he rose to it and gained his independence and maturity, with no loss of Christian conviction or devotion, marking the change from the child to the man. Like Eden, one of the harrowing steps to maturity was the loss of an elder brother in France in the on-going carnage of the trenches.

Alfred enlisted as 'Private no.4541 A T Houghton' on 4 April 1916. Like many recruits before and since, he was formed up in a squad with some twenty others, marched to a train and from the station to Taunton barracks, under the direction of a recruiting sergeant. His army issue clothing included khaki tunic and trousers, black boots, puttees and a cap with a Somerset Light Infantry badge, along with a water bottle and an entrenching tool and heavy khaki great-coat. A spell in Bournemouth included a standard TAB injection, which caused a number of his colleagues to faint and gave him a bad reaction, before all were drafted to Winchester and a tented camp at Hursley Park, five miles out of the city. Here they were in the charge of a fine looking, tall corporal with a West Somerset accent, which Alfred liked to hear, and were roused at 6.30am. Alfred determined to maintain his own Christian discipline, would read his Daily Light in bed before reveille 'my spiritual *hors d'oevres* to begin the day'. A parade at 7am was followed by a queue for breakfast with his mess tin. Somehow, after this meal, he found opportunity to sit on a bench for his daily Quiet Time before a further parade at 9am.

Sunday mornings meant a compulsory church parade for all; but Alfred added to that a visit to the village church at Hursley in the evening. There is no sign of an awareness that this had been John Keble's church, connected through him to the rise of the Oxford Movement, where he had gone to be incumbent three years after his Assize Sermon, seen often as the beginning of the movement in 1833. Alfred's main memory was the loss of a pair of good kid gloves, left on a pew and never seen again. He remembered also having a silver topped cane, to be placed under the arm in order to salute a passing officer. In early June 1916 his company commander gave him leave in response to a telegram from his father, telling him that Herbert was home for 48 hours from his camp in Sittingbourne in Kent with the Queen's regiment preparatory to a posting to France. Herbert too had identified himself with the local church and was known as a Christian in his unit. Their shared experience in uniform led to lengthy late night discussion. Herbert revealed that his fiancée, Laura Sparkshott, daughter of a CMS missionary in the Sudan, had broken off their engagement, which, though a very bitter blow, freed him from one major anxiety as he faced service at the front with an intuition that he would not survive. He was indeed killed in the Somme offensive on 3 July 1916. His brother wrote that their meeting on June 6th was 'the last time I saw Herbert on earth'.

Alfred's initial reaction to news of Herbert's death was to be stunned and then to rebel against the God who had allowed it to happen: why should a united family be broken up in this way? Why? Why? He spent the night after receiving the telegram from his father on sentry duty with time to reflect and this was followed by a 'miserable weekend', 'utterly repudiating the will of God in bringing disaster on me and my family'. In this despondent and rebellious mood he walked five miles into Winchester to Christ Church, an evangelical church known to him, but nothing in the service helped his state, until a verse (John 18:11) came to him: 'the cup which my Father has given me, shall I not drink it?'

In April 1915 he had attended a convention meeting in Bath, addressed by two well-known speakers of the Keswick Convention, one of whom was Prebendary Webb-Peploe. In view of Alfred's later service on the Keswick Council, it is interesting to notice that his father had grave doubts about the Keswick emphases, regarded as suspect, Arminian and heretical. Frank and Alfred had still gone to the meetings, where Webb-Peploe had addressed war-time bereavement, which he knew he might himself confront in his own sons at the front. He had described various Christian responses to the will of God, from sad acceptance to what he saw as an ultimate stage, when even in his bitter suffering in Gethsemane, Christ had accepted the cup of suffering, not reluctantly, but as 'the good and acceptable will of God'. To Webb-Peploe, Jesus' response in John 18:11 was a joyful response to the will of a loving Father, which could only lead to good. This memory acted with the impact of a personal revelation to Alfred in the context of Herbert's death: 'I came out of church a changed man and the Lord flooded my soul with joy': even Herbert's death could be transfigured (and many subsequent disasters and bereavements) seen in the light of this understanding.

Like so many young men, Herbert had 'gone over the top' at 7am on the morning of July 3rd. Shot in the leg, he had dropped into a shell hole. When he raised his head to look out, he was shot and died instantly. He had written a moving letter to his father and mother dated 1 July 1916, assuring them of his love for the whole family: 'if you get news of my death in action it will not be long before we shall all meet again in heaven.... Don't be sad if I am killed but rejoice in the victory of our armies, because our cause is a righteous one. I shall be proud and glad to die in such a cause'. After ending with 'au revoir' he had added a postscript on Sunday evening July 2nd: '(I) have just heard that we shall go into action tomorrow (Monday July 3rd) morning. Best love to you all once more. HH'. A private from the Sittingbourne camp wrote to his father of his godly, unselfish influence and conscientious work 'proud to have known such a splendid fellow'. The day after Alfred's experience at Christ Church, he learned that he was to join a draft to Burma. Again, he was given special permission for leave to see his family, who travelled to Hursley, before his embarkation.

He sailed on the SS Ceramic, a White Star liner which had been converted into a troopship. His father arranged for him to have the Times Weekly while abroad and supplied him with a weekly sermon, often one of Charles Spurgeon's, for his spiritual nurture. The officer in charge of the draft invited him to be an acting lance-corporal for the duration of the voyage 'my first Army responsibility'. He bought a copy of Palgrave's *Golden Treasury* in Plymouth to accompany the voyage. As they cast off, from the Devonport docks, Plymouth Hoe was crowded with people waving to them. An escort of two destroyers went with the liner. After the Bay of Biscay and the Straits of Gibraltar, they were attacked in the Mediterranean by German U-boats on July 26, 1916: as Alfred slept on deck 'I was aware of an ear-splitting crack as shells passed over the ship', his first experience of being under fire. It was fortunate for all on board (Alfred reckoned that the provision of life-boats was inadequate for the numbers) that the torpedoes fired at the liner missed their target; he learned later that the barman had been so sure that the ship would be sunk that he had offered the officers present free drinks, among whom was Major (later Field Marshal) Bill Slim, who was to tell Alfred this story on their return by ship to Liverpool. After Valetta harbour in Malta they proceeded to Port Said and the Suez Canal, when khaki drill and solar topees became the uniform for the tropics, the headgear being prescribed as obligatory from one hour after sunrise till one hour before sunset, a rule he kept until 1946: 'I fully believed that the most dire consequences might ensue – sunstroke and death – if one broke this rule!'

The Red Sea was 'tremendously hot' but in the Indian Ocean they struck the monsoon before reaching Bombay (Mumbai) on August 13,1916, providing him with his first experience of the east, with its low-lying coastline and palm trees. Railway carriages were drawn up at the docks, with the slatted wooden seats of the third class carriage on Indian railways, in which they travelled for three days to Calcutta before marching to Fort William barracks on the Ganges River. Alfred was able to make contact with a friend and family from Victoria College days, an Anglo-Indian family called Cosserat, who entertained him in the luxury of the Bristol Hotel in Calcutta: Mrs Cosserat also introduced him to the Hindu temple, Khali Ghat, after which the city was named and he visited the Maidan and the famous street of Chowringhee. He found the idol in the temple 'hideous' and it left him with 'a sense of evil and the power of Satan'. Three to four days later he embarked on a small boat to Rangoon but the combination of the monsoon, the smell of goats in the hold near to his sleeping quarters and the general discomfort induced violent sea-sickness.

Alfred's first arrival in Burma up the Rangoon River was to experience a country treated as an extension of the British Raj in India. In 1885 the British had invaded Burma (Myanmar today) and exiled its ruler, King Thibaw, replacing ancient Burmese tradition and government with their own alien methods, resented by the Burmese people. As far as missionary work was concerned, in which one day Alfred would embark, Adoniram Judson (1788-1850), the American Baptist, had been a great pioneer among the Karen people in the nineteenth century and translated the Bible into Burmese.

The Church of England had begun to work among Burmese in the 1850s and during this visit Alfred met with Kachin people, to whom ultimately he would go as a missionary, in what was a predominantly Buddhist and animist context. For now, the country and its people attracted him at once, though he found it hard to tell men and women apart: both wore turbans, jackets and 'longyis' or skirts going down to the ankles. The SLI had companies at Mandalay, Shwebo and Meiktila and Alfred joined the last of these. His quarters were in a traditional bungalow on stilts constructed from teak pillars, six by six inches square, with brick or concrete bases. A staircase led to a wide verandah which in turn led on to a large and long room with iron cots down either wall and a teak roof.

After a rebuke on the parade ground from the RSM for failing to stand to attention when addressed, Alfred was ordered to see the adjutant. This was the same Captain Pulman who had been so impressed with his fielding at Victoria College and who now told him that he had put his name down for the Officer Cadet Unit at Sialkot, then in the Indian Punjab, for January 1917. Before this four month course began, Alfred had time to explore Burmese conditions, including a visit to a pagoda, where he conversed with a Buddhist priest who spoke some English, took a photo of him and gave him a copy of St Mark's gospel. He found that troops attending church parades always carried rifles and five rounds of live ammunition, a practice which stemmed from a massacre at a church during the Indian Mutiny (Sepoy Rebellion) of 1857. He was confronted with a Welsh chaplain who was a convinced Anglo-Catholic, later an archdeacon of Rangoon, who wore Eucharistic vestments and used wafers for communion, associated in the minds of many evangelicals with unacceptable views on transubstantiation in Alfred's day; despite the man's friendliness, Alfred 'went once but never again', while having theological arguments with him as opportunity arose. He was classed as a first class shot in this period (he just failed the highest category of marksman) and experienced a Christmas Dinner when by tradition the officers waited on the men and there was free beer ('which I did not take'). Back in the bungalow he joined in a festive duet.

On New Year's Day 1917 he left Rangoon, joined a party of other potential officers and, after three days in Calcutta, he reached Sialkot which he found bitterly cold in his tropical khaki drill. There were 150 cadets in training all from Territorial regiments. They learned 'mess etiquette' suitable to officers and gentlemen and a group of them formed a Gilbert and Sullivan singing group, with a certain Sutton Jones as their pianist, an ex-chorister from Exeter Cathedral, who also had a good tenor voice, with an older man called Blower, an old Etonian with a deep bass voice who loved to sing 'When your heart is in your boots, tarantara', and others. Alfred quickly became a Gilbert and Sullivan addict, enjoying the humour and musical combinations which 'gave me a tremendous kick', though he thought his father would have disapproved. To the question to which regiment he wished to be commissioned he replied the SLI, to whom he had 'lost my heart' with their short, fast step and rifles at the trail rather than shouldered. He was gazetted as second lieutenant on 28 April 1917. A letter from King George V reached his father and referred to 'our trusty and beloved Alfred Thomas Houghton', commissioned into the 5th Battalion Prince Albert's (Somerset Light Infantry).

Sutton Jones, the singer, gave Alfred the advice, that were he to find himself at Kirkee, five miles from Poona (Pune) he should look for a family called Gardner who, among other things to commend them, had three attractive daughters. In due course Alfred was to form a strong attachment to the oldest of the three, Dorothy, a source of much heartache later in the war. Meanwhile, he learned of various happenings at home, notably his father's move to Whitington in Norfolk aged 58, perhaps welcome after his earlier breakdown and Frank's curacy at St Benedict's, Everton in Liverpool: he too had experienced a breakdown during his training at Highbury, helped through it by a sympathetic member of staff, whom Alfred however viewed as over liberal in theological outlook if pastorally supportive.

Newly Commissioned 2nd Lieutenant Tim Houghton
In Muttra, India, 1917

Frank had faced the reluctance of Bishop Chavasse of Liverpool to ordain anyone of military age and apparent fitness to serve, as the father of two sons on active service, one of whom won two VC's for outstanding gallantry, the second VC being posthumous. Although Frank had been declared unfit for military service by a doctor, Chavasse required a second opinion before he would agree to ordain. Stanley followed his brothers to Clarence School in 1917 and Lydia (Biddy) and Freda went to Bath High School, from where Lydia moved into her medical studies at Bristol University. As he reached his majority, becoming 21 in 1917, Alfred was happy to have achieved a life long ambition to join the army, despite his long-term missionary calling, and was able to 'thank God for my upbringing and even for the strict discipline involved', although he was aware that at certain points he was breaking loose from the inhibitions of the past. What, however, might apply to Gilbert and Sullivan ('anathema to my father') did not apply to ecclesiastical practices like vestments and wafers, 'where my father's teaching still kept a grip on me'. He sensed too that God might have some purpose in bringing him to India but was still very unsure where he might eventually serve.

As an infantry officer Alfred's pay increased from £27 p.a. to £270 and he also had the services of a batman/bearer in Ibrahim. Among other accomplishments, Ibrahim was able to tie Alfred's bow tie for evenings in the mess, where he was expected to wear a mess jacket, dress shirt, black bow-tie and a cummerbund in regimental colours, which meant black and gold. For early morning parades Ibrahim helped him into his boots and puttees before 6.30am: in temperatures of 115 degrees, military duties were over by 9am. Alfred suffered excessively from prickly heat, which Ibrahim treated with a block of ice for his back as relief. As a teetotaller he was faced with such issues as the loyal toast, when the port was passed around from the president. He decided that, as he drank fermented wine at Holy Communion, he could drink enough for a toast when the cry 'Gentlemen, the King Emperor' was made. He took a course in equestrianism at the local Remounts Depot. He disliked the experience but learned enough to become riding master in the mission in Burma long afterwards.

After periods in Muttra and Bangalore (200 feet above sea level and so a cure for his prickly heat) he was sent to the SLI battalion in Peshawar. He travelled via Agra, from where he visited the Taj Mahal and marvelled at it, and on through Lahore and Rawalpindi, only to be told in Peshawar that the SLI battalion had moved to Dinapur. This unit was ordered to Palestine, which might have fulfilled his long held wish to be engaged in an active theatre, but Simla judged that he and another officer called Waterson would be supernumerary to requirements, a great disappointment to him. Instead, the two were posted to a camp near Poona at Kirkee. This led him to follow up Sutton Jones' suggestion that he should try to make contact with the Gardner family and their three daughters.

The Gardner girls attended a convent school in Poona. They were Dorothy aged 17½, Marjorie (15) and Joan (12), described as 'vivacious, attractive and pretty girls'. As a friend of Sutton Jones, Alfred found the family immediately welcoming and their family life of instant appeal, the first family he had known since leaving England. Mrs Gardner became an alternative mother figure to him. Dorothy, like her mother, was open, hospitable with 'an affectionate laugh'. Alfred was invited to spend his Christmas leave with them in a tented area. Here, at her request, he read poetry to Dorothy and their relationship developed. At his suggestion Dorothy joined the Scripture Union and he found her a ready listener on spiritual subjects. Alfred was then ordered to Secunderabad in February 1918: on the train journey from Poona, he lay on a top bunk of a first class carriage, matched to his officer status, and realised that he was deeply in love with this girl and yet separated from her. He was aware that, although willing enough to be the wife of a clergyman, Dorothy did not favour his plans for missionary work. He wrote to his parents, singing her praises, but received a highly dampening reply, filled with apprehension and anxiety about any turning from his missionary calling. Nevertheless, having prayed earnestly that they might be reunited he was overjoyed when the opportunity for a posting back to Kirkee became possible and daily visits to the Gardner home with it. Another posting to Secunderabad followed with many army experiences, while he kept in touch with Dorothy at a distance, but in November 1919 he made a final visit to the Gardner home before returning to England. A first and deep romantic relationship seems to have ended then but not without some personal agonies over the loss.

The barracks at Secunderabad, which Alfred joined in the reserve battalion, was commanded by a Roman Catholic major, for whom Alfred had a great respect as a soldier and with whom he had many discussions on religion. Plainly, the major admired him in return and when a request came from army head-quarters in Simla by telegram that a 'young, keen, gentlemanly, intelligent officer' was needed as a staff officer to the Inspector of Infantry (south), Brigadier General W C Walton, the major gave Alfred 'his tight lipped grin' and said 'I have decided to send you, Houghton'. A telegram was composed commending Alfred as an 'outstanding officer' with many other commendatory adjectives, which, rather to his chagrin, Alfred was deputed to send at his own expense: as it was long and sent on Sunday when rates were doubled, it came to a large sum. No reimbursement was offered.

He travelled from Secunderabad to Bombay and arrived at his new posting in Jhansi a day before his new chief, General Walton. Alfred was not without regrets over his new appointment as, despite many attractions, it was a final bar to active service. He discovered soon that he was both staff officer and ADC to the general, with responsibility for arranging complicated rail journeys and draft programmes for the inspections at varied sites. He also had to deal with the cook on their train and ensure that the general, who was markedly abstemious, still received his White Horse whiskey for a single whisky and soda with his dinner. Alfred found the general to be 'a man of the highest integrity, thoroughly self-disciplined and conscientious', who worked hard and expected him to do the same. To keep fit, the general both rode horses and bicycled: Alfred had been instructed to buy a bicycle to accompany him. In Poona they were entertained by the brigade commander, General Norrie (with only one arm), and Lady Norrie 'a very gracious hostess' who always addressed Alfred (wrongly) as 'Captain Houghton'. His introduction by General Walton to all and sundry ran 'my staff officer, who has no vices: he neither drinks nor smokes'. In 1918 there was a flu epidemic which was reckoned to have killed more people than the Great War itself: 600 per day were dying in Bombay. Alfred caught the infection and was sent to hospital in a bullock 'tonga', despite a high temperature and a splitting headache. He was greeted by an Australian nurse, who found he had a temperature of 105° but she managed to get it down during the night. Still weak from flu he was ordered back to duty to meet the GOC and spent a miserable day on a large black horse which he was quite unable to control, one of the worst days of his life.

He and the general spent some time in Simla, the army's cooler base for the Delhi headquarters and in use from November to March. He enjoyed membership of the United Services Club and approved their custom of ending a meal with a slice of Madeira cake and a glass of port. He attended the garrison church, where he found the Viceroy (Lord Chelmsford) and the Commander in Chief (Sir Charles Munro) with many others present. His pay now rose to 680 Rs. (£544) on the GSO 2 grade (General Staff Officer). As General Walton's area for inspections included all India and Burma, the Punjab and NorthWest Frontier only excepted, Alfred was aware that he toured the countries at the army's expense. He took the opportunity to visit CMS, MMS and American Methodist missions and Mrs Gardner arranged for him to visit Mukti (meaning Deliverance), the orphanage home run by the famous Pandita Ramabai, 30 miles from Poona. Despite her age and deafness at sixty, he was impressed by the work and the influence of George Müller and Hudson Taylor upon it, with the same view that God would provide funding in response to faith. Agnes, his sister, sent him the first volume of Hudson Taylor's life, *The Growth of a Soul* prior to an inspection trip in Burma and he wrote that 'it had a profound effect on me'. This and 'the laughter loving people' of Burma, a country he preferred to India, may have begun to shape his missionary calling further. It was during this trip that he met Kachins for the first time: but at this stage he reflected that as the missionaries among them were either American or Baptist it was difficult to see how he could serve amongst them: 'I was left with my stirrings and the assurance that if God wanted me there He would open the door' even if, speaking humanly, it seemed 'utterly impossible'.

Alfred's continuing tours of India and Burma continued. The journey which led to the Kachins included Meiktila, Mandalay, a trip along the Irrawaddy to Annapurna and on by train to Bhamo, where he found that the engine was fired with wood as fuel. A further river trip involved the Brahmaputra into Assam, and there were visits to Hyderabad and Karachi. Back in Delhi the building of New Delhi was in process, including the massive vice-regal palace designed, with its surrounding buildings, by Sir Edwin Lutyens. Alfred found that 'everyone took it all as a big and expensive joke' and he wrote that even Lutyens himself referred to his colleagues in the work as 'fellow comedians'. When they left Delhi again for Simla, Alfred was able to stay with another hospitable family, the Humes, which became memorable because the son of the family called him 'facetiously' 'Timothy Titus'. He wrote: 'the name Timothy has stuck to me ever since' and 'most people imagine that my real name is 'Tim''. As he disliked Alfred Thomas, he was only too willing to collude.

Passing through Allahabad on one of his many train journeys, he bought a newspaper which announced the Armistice on 11ᵗʰ November 1918. He imagined at once that the inspection arranged for that day would be cancelled: the military mind however was undisturbed by such news and the parade continued as usual. By 1919 there was widespread unrest in India and growing resentment against the British, only enhanced by the action of General Dyer in firing on defenceless civilians in Amritsar. While this action, after due warnings, was condemned then and since by many commentators, it is interesting to find that those on the ground believed, Alfred among them, that Dyer's decision saved thousands of lives of Europeans, once more, in their view, under threat. His host, Colonel Hume, 'no warmonger', proved 'profoundly thankful for the action that had been taken'. The case raised a furore both at home and in India, but, though it was discussed in parliament, to the disgust and outrage of Indian opinion the House of Lords refused to censure Dyer.

Before leaving India, Alfred still had occasions of great interest to experience back in Simla. He met the Gough family, Canon Gough being CMS secretary for the Punjab and father of Hugh Gough, whom Alfred was to know as a Keswick speaker, as Bishop of Barking and later Archbishop of Sydney and with whom he collaborated in the early days of what became the Church of England Evangelical Council in 1946, a body he later chaired. He relieved his boredom in an office job by reading the Bhagavad Gita and attended a missionary convention addressed by the famous Methodist missionary, E Stanley Jones. Still more memorable to him was a meeting with Sadhu Sundar Singh in Simla: 'here was a Christ like character, if ever there was one'. Alfred was aware of the patronising attitudes of many Europeans towards Indians and aware that to some degree he shared them; but felt at once that any such attitude with the Sadhu was entirely inappropriate: ' in looks and dress he appeared very much what one might imagine Jesus would be like on earth. He wore the saffron coloured robe and turban of a sadhu… his expression was gentle and kind and his eyes compelled attention. I felt I was in the presence of a holy man of God'. The Sadhu was equally at home with a Tibetan hillman on the roadside or speaking to 'a crowd of thousands of people'. For Alfred 'I regard it as one of the great privileges of my life to have met Sadhu Sundar Singh'. A sign of older attitudes had been revealed when E. Stanley Jones had suggested that Europeans should be willing to serve under their Indian brethren: 'I remember one little missionary, with a beard, literally shaking his fist in Stanley Jones' face at his temerity in making such a suggestion', which as Alfred wrote, later in the century was regarded as a commonplace.

Once more the possibility of active service was held out to him when General Walton was given a brigade command on the north-west frontier and offered to take him to fight the Afghans. He knew, however, that the war proper for which he had enlisted was now over since November 1918: 'a higher law now operated. God had graciously allowed me to fulfil my ambition for military service but He had called me to be a missionary and to the (ordained) ministry. I had no right therefore to prolong my stay in the Army by embarking on an adventure which might hold me up.....'. He saw himself as a man under authority. Before leaving he attended a final occasion at the vice-regal lodge in Simla with Lord and Lady Chelmsford, soon after which his demobilisation papers arrived with orders to report to Bombay. He had time for two fleeting visits to the Gardner family and Dorothy, from whom he found it 'hard to leave' for 'all the old longings came back'; but, after one more night in camp, he boarded the SS Guildford Castle, paying off his latest bearer, Abdul, who was in tears, and finding a late arrival in Major William Slim, who had been a subaltern on the Ceramic but with whom Alfred was now a fellow officer returning to Liverpool: 'it came to me with great force that the Lord had watched over me all these war years, when the future seemed completely uncertain and now I was going home to prepare myself for the Lord's service, whatever that should be'.

CHAPTER 3

TRAINING FOR SERVICE

The journey home to Liverpool included time spent in the company of the future Field Marshal Sir William Slim. Alfred learned that he was a Roman Catholic, who had been educated at Stonyhurst with a view to becoming a Jesuit priest but he told Alfred that 'they gave him up in the end as he was unwilling to be broken' which Alfred felt to be 'a very interesting illustration'. Through Slim he was introduced to the RC chaplain on board, who told him that he prayed for him daily 'as a heretic'. Slim, Alfred, the chaplain and some others made up a syndicate to buy some vintage Madeira which Slim discovered on board and all enjoyed a nightly glass on deck before retiring. On a more serious note, Alfred had persuaded the captain of the vessel to have church parades on Sundays, so long as these were kept short: he gave ten minute talks on such subjects as 'What is truth?' or 'What is faith?'. The ship reached Port Said on Armistice Day (11 November 1919) and Alfred reflected how he had moved from private to staff captain in 3½ years, the last appointment being gazetted on 5 June 1919, and that his pay of £1000 p.a. was not matched until he became general secretary of BCMS in the 1950's, by which time the value of money meant that it was worth very much less than in 1919. He and an officer called Oakley took a boat ashore to celebrate the Armistice together at a Port Said restaurant, Oakley proposing a bottle of Sauterne for the occasion, which Alfred shared with him but 'that bottle of Sauterne was the last intoxicating drink I ever shared in'.

They arrived at Liverpool on November 26th in bitterly cold conditions. Here he met with Frank, by then serving as curate at All Saints, Preston, having accompanied his vicar when E.M. Benson left St. Benedict's, Liverpool. Their very different experiences since leaving school made Alfred think that 'they were strangers to one another'. Neither had he seen his father's new setting at Whitington in Norfolk, which today since his father's time has been spelled Whittington. He had a difficult cross country train journey before arriving at Downham Market, to find his father on the platform, who took him for tea in the town 'the most delicious I could ever remember'. On the local train connection, they met an adjutant called Duffield, also recently demobilised, who had been led to Christian faith by Alfred's father. On arrival at their station the verger (Mr Reeves) put Alfred's luggage in a hand-cart, which he wheeled towards the church and vicarage, where Alfred found his mother and sister Freda in 'an atmosphere of oil lamps, candles, and water daily pumped up to the scullery from an underground well'. He went to bed exhausted and slept until the following noon.

It was an opportunity to visit family, using his army rail passes on the trains: first to Agnes in Bath, who was acting as a companion to an elderly lady, member of a Plymouth Brethren assembly; next to Stanley, who was teaching as an assistant master at Monkton Combe Junior School at Combe Down; then Lydia, now a medical student at Bristol University; and finally again in Preston, where he spoke to Frank's class of boys, who included a young Ian Isherwood, one day to be Home Secretary of CMS, and George Scott, Frank's special protégé, who, after serving as a missionary in China with CIM, became the Home Director of the mission later.

As he had already reached the canonical age for ordination of 23, Alfred was understandably keen to proceed through his training as speedily as possible. He heard that Oxford and Cambridge were offering 'fast track' degrees for service personnel. London University, for which he had qualified, was considering such concessions when he applied to St John's, Highbury and was accepted by the principal for the BD course. The college dated from 1863, when a wealthy evangelical, Alfred Peache, had been convinced of the need for an evangelical theological college at a meeting addressed by a Fellow of St John's College, Cambridge, T P Boultbee, when Peache was an incumbent of Margotsfield. Peache had offered to find the money for the foundation and Boultbee became the first principal (G R Balleine, *A History of the Evangelical Party in the Church of England* (1951) p.217). Meanwhile Alfred was seeking concessions from the senate of the university but found that, at very short notice, he was faced with compulsory Hebrew. This decided him to follow the example of a number of men in the college, who were pursuing a L.Th in Durham, the first year of which could be done at Highbury, with a second in Durham University.

Alfred found settling down to study in 1921 after his years in the army very difficult and initially felt that he used the college in London as a convenient jumping-off ground for meeting friends in town. Letters arrived for him addressed to Captain A T Houghton or Captain Tim Houghton, the name he had acquired while staying with the Humes in India. Although his father and mother continued to call him Alfred, from now on he was known as Tim or 'AT' by his own wish throughout his adult life, a change of styling which will be observed in this text. Meanwhile, he assessed the college staff perceptively: A W Greenup, the principal, who was rarely seen, was however both scholarly and godly and his sermons in chapel 'simple and biblical'. The vice-principal, Dr Harden, was a warm-hearted Irishman who later became Bishop of Tuam, not as conservative as Tim preferred but no radical either. Of the others, Dr J N Carpenter was the young teacher who had helped Frank and exercised wide influence in the student body but Tim was theologically *en garde*, fearing what he saw as liberalism. By contrast, Dodgson Sykes, the dean, was a known conservative but seen by conservative students to 'sit on the fence when any controversy arose between liberal and conservative evangelical students'. At this stage Sykes was a confirmed bachelor, living in rooms over the college's gateway, but he was recognised as a good theological coach, not least on the New Testament, who also played soccer, cricket and tennis with the students. His marriage, noticed later in Tim's writings, was to produce, in his son Stephen, a future theological professor, first in Durham and then in Cambridge, who moved on the be Bishop of Ely and Principal of St John's College, Durham.

This college was a sister foundation to St John's, Highbury and the choice of a number of Tim's friends who wanted to do their final year of the L.Th in Durham (Note: the Trust Deed of the Council of Highbury read: 'St John's Hall Highbury has a branch in Durham called St John's Hall … students who spend two years at Highbury have the privilege of admission to the Hall at Durham in preference to other students' cf. G C B Davies, *Men for the Ministry*, p. 59). Charles Wallis, the principal of the time, had moved from Highbury where he had served before the war and Tim regarded him as 'genial', even if his view of the college was that its evangelicalism was 'less definite' than Highbury. Along with other friends, he decided that he would prefer, as an act of Christian witness, to leave the confines of another theological college and (as was allowed) do his final year (1922) at University College, Durham which occupied Durham Castle. Meanwhile he had to complete his year at Highbury, a pattern which included daily morning and evening prayer and in his case also attendance at a Missionary Prayer Meeting before the first, known as 'Vigiles'. He assisted at St Paul's, Canonbury and its mission hall in Wakeham Street, where he helped to start children's work, which developed to 200 or so and a meeting for some 30 adults. This with open air meetings outside pubs, he found 'very tough going' but also 'a grand preparation for the future as I realised that human resources were utterly useless apart from the enabling power of the Holy Spirit'. Human hearts were hard and unresponsive, he discovered.

Of his old friends and acquaintances from India, he met again General Walton, fresh from the Afghan War, and, at his flat in Thurlow Place, even helped to polish the buttons on the uniform to be worn at an investiture at Buckingham Palace. He entertained Dorothy Gardner to tea in London, now training as a nurse at Bart's; by then however 'our minds were now pretty far apart' and, although the past was 'a lovely dream', they had decided that they were no longer meant for one another. More significant for his future was his meeting with the youngest student at Highbury, Bryan Green, 'a most dynamic character', who involved Tim in the boys' work about which he was so enthusiastic and drew him out ('I owe a tremendous debt to him for bringing me out of my spiritual shell'), sharing views on college staff and the student body. Tim had been persuaded to join the LIFCU (London Inter-Faculty Christian Union) which, with the CICCU (Cambridge Inter-Collegiate Christian Union), were to provide the nucleus of the new IVF, founded in 1920, and which one day Tim would serve as a travelling secretary. The embryonic IVF had a house-party at the Keswick Convention of July 1920 and Bryan Green and Tim were invited and decided to attend. By then Tim had already been intrigued by a photograph of Bryan's sister on the mantelpiece of his study at Highbury. The Keswick plan involved a visit to the Green family home in Upper

Norwood. The 'lovely and very attractive face' of the photograph, which belonged to Coralie Green, opened the door of the Green household on their arrival, but with her hair 'bobbed' and so looking very much younger in the flesh: nevertheless his interest remained. He was made very welcome in the Green home and learned that Mr Green's father had been a general in India, as well as tennis singles champion there in his day. The family invited 'Captain Houghton' to escort Coralie and her two school friends with Bryan to fireworks at the Crystal Palace that evening: 'in the crowds there had to be a lot of escorting and holding of arms and though Captain Houghton tried to be impartial, he certainly found himself thrown into the company of Coralie Mary more than anyone else'. So began a romance which, by the time he wrote this sentence, had lasted 58 years through marriage and resulted in 21 grandchildren at that date.

At Keswick, Dr Algy Stanley-Smith, son of one of the Cambridge Seven which had included C.T. Studd in 1885, was their house parent, by then himself a CMS missionary in Uganda and about to pioneer in Ruanda. Both Godfrey Buxton, son of the vicar Barclay Buxton, and Clarence Foster were fellow guests, both of them then Cambridge undergraduates, though Buxton was still suffering from severe war wounds on his legs from the trenches in France. Once more Prebendary Webb-Peploe was a speaker at the convention, as was the well known Baptist F.B. Meyer and Bishop Taylor Smith, who had acted as chaplain general to the forces. Others included Stuart Holden, whom Tim had gone to hear in his church of St Paul's, Portman Square with appreciation, Dr. Graham Scroggie and the authority on Islam and missionary to Muslims, Dr. Samuel Zwemer. For Tim the effect of Keswick was to underline two realities: first, that his earlier sense of isolation as a committed believer was dissipated; and secondly, the need for total surrender to God and His will. This last caused him to sever some relationships which he felt to be a distraction from single-minded service to God 'making a clean cut of everything which came between me and God'. Crusader camp at Felixstowe followed Keswick, a valuable introduction to boys' work, although he noted wryly that a Crusader leader who insisted on talking personally to every boy 'did much harm as a result'. He was able to learn from the mistakes, as well as the strengths, of such bodies.

To his surprise, late in 1920 Frank his brother offered to CIM and preceded him to the mission field, when the family had assumed, and Tim with them, that Frank was committed to the ministry at home. He went to serve with Bishop W W Cassels, another of the original Cambridge Seven, in Liangshau, which lay in the diocese of Szechwan (Sichuan) of which Cassels was the first bishop. In a letter of 30 January 1921 (replying to one of Tim's of 13 December 1920) Frank showed his awareness of missionary realities in what Tim described as a 'prophetic' statement: 'most missionaries seem to think that real *friendship* between ourselves and the Chinese is impossible, or, if possible, unhealthy. Naturally, my heart revolts against such a theory. In any case I am sure they are far more lovable than I expected'. It was over ten years since the Indian Christian leader V S Azariah had made his famous appeal at the world missionary conference at Edinburgh of 1910, which had ended 'we ask for love: *give us friends*' in a stirring address: plainly the lesson was only slowly being learned. Frank had asked Tim to pray for him to find a wife. Tim later met Bishop Cassels' daughter, Dorrie, and had thought how suitable she might be: Frank did indeed marry her on 12 July 1923 in Paoning (Langzhong), the cathedral city, where he was principal of a small theological college, after earlier serving as headmaster of a boys' school.

Tim's own romance with Coralie was helped forward by visits to the Green home in Michaelmas 1920, when he and Bryan were planning a boys' campaign for Sydenham in the Christmas holidays. Coralie, still a schoolgirl of 16, got his help with her homework and he discovered had surreptitiously cleaned the bicycle that he had brought for the campaign later. Coralie herself had attended a Children's Special Service Mission (CSSM), led by Clifford Martin, later Bishop of Liverpool and at the time president of the CICCU. One of the leaders was Max Warren's elder brother, Jack, who was to die young as a missionary in Uganda: through Jack Warren, Coralie had deepened her Christian conversion of earlier in the year (dated 1 January 1920) at the party and was now a keen member of the Crusaders' Union and aware of a possible missionary calling. Tim and Coralie took part together in a CSSM at St Leonard's-on-Sea, where Bryan Green took a leading part, and, after staying with the Greens following the mission, Tim felt that he and Coralie were 'pledged to each other', although, with Coralie still at school aged 17, a formal engagement was not announced. After his earlier experience with Dorothy (which he had shared with Coralie) Tim was circumspect about broaching the subject at home. When he did, once more he received a dampening response from his mother as she stood at the sink in Whitington Vicarage: *not that girl*'. He felt that, had he produced a quiet female with no interest in her appearance and 'a bun on the back of her head' his mother would have responded more warmly. Coralie's bobbed hair and vivacity may have appeared immodest to his mother, whereas in fact 'there could not be anyone more modest and womanly, hating to push herself forward and always underestimating her gifts'. By contrast the Greens welcomed the engagement and, slowly his own parents accepted Coralie, who stayed at Whitington.

While he was at the CSSM he had been approached by a church warden of Holy Trinity, Tunbridge Wells, a Colonel Caudy, about serving a curacy with Barclay Buxton, a former CMS missionary in Japan and founder of the Japan Evangelistic Band, whose son Godfrey had been at Keswick. Tim decided to get ordained before his final year's study at Durham for the L.Th and to work in the parish as a deacon during his vacations. He was ordained by Bishop Harmer in Rochester Cathedral on 21 December 1921. Barclay Buxton gave him the children's work in the parish to develop, with an opportunity to lead a mission to all the town's Sunday Schools during a series of meetings in the Christmas vacation.

His ordination as deacon was unhappy, in contrast to the later one for his priesting. He admitted with some honesty that he 'had not much use for parsons as a class'. He determined to retain his military moustache and in a further offence to authority refused to buy a white stole in addition to cassock and surplice, or to turn east for the creed during the services on the retreat. The combination of the silence, little food and a spiritual diet of little value to him meant that for him it was a 'miserable time of semi-martyrdom or at least feeling like a fish out of water'. All this was further compacted by an interview with the bishop over the wearing of a stole. The bishop appealed to his oath of canonical obedience, to which he replied 'Yes, my lord, in all things lawful and honest' which in his view did not include wearing a stole. 'I think you are very petty' was the bishop's parting reply and Tim well remembered the look of horror on the archdeacon's face, confronted by a candidate but no stole to drape round his shoulder. He commented: 'I had felt like a martyr of the Inquisition at an *auto-da-fé* and my ordination which should have been such a blessing, was an utter misery'. A broad smile from the bishop as he handed him his Letters of Orders with a warm handshake did much to allay his depression and, after this evidence of allowing bygones to be bygones, 'I went away feeling quite elated'.

His curacy, as with many, produced mixed experiences. Barclay Buxton would meet with his curates on Monday morning and Tim could always be assured of lunch at the vicarage. His landlady, a tall, kindly and elderly lady with rooms at 50, York Rd., Tunbridge Wells warned him of the many young ladies of the parish whose mothers would be delighted to marry them off to an attractive young curate. He found that his Sunday School campaign was indeed well supplied with such 'desirable maidens', among them the future wife of Max Warren, who became general secretary of CMS later, Mary Collett. On his first Sunday he assisted at the 8am Holy Communion, after which the vicar asked him to take a wedding immediately. The legality of this on a Sunday in the 1920's was doubtful and diaconal weddings always an ecclesiastical exception if not irregularity, but assisted by the verger he plunged into the marriage service to which the vicar had pointed him in the vestry. The service was completed between communion and breakfast in his digs. With a minimum of preparation and advice it was a high test. Sundays were in any case a trial of endurance. After the 8am he had two ward services regularly in a hospital, 11am next, followed by an afternoon service for 'maids' which was a hangover from the previous regime of Canon Hoare, resented by the curates, which they eventually managed to get dropped. He either then preached at or led evening prayer at 6.30 but on alternate Sundays this was preceded by a half hour service at a Homeopathic Hospital with no remission of evensong after doing it. An after-church evangelistic service was introduced based on the parish's Crabbe Institute, which became an open air in summer months. He had a regular pattern of 7 or 8 engagements. It was a daunting programme and, although he only preached once a month in the parish church in theory, he had many other addresses weekly.

The academic year of 1922 was spent in Durham. By choosing to go to University College, he found that he had rooms in the castle keep. Buckets of coal were provided for open fires and, although he got his own breakfast, lunch and dinner were held in the medieval hall of the castle. Dinners were formal meals with a high table procession and a long Latin grace. Waiters then provided soup, meat, dessert and coffee: no one was permitted to leave until the high table had departed. He hardly met the Master, Ellershaw, but had more to do with the Bursar 'Major MacFarlane'. The recent history of the university *The Durham Difference* (2007) gives him his full title of Colonel Angus MacFarlane Grieve, a central figure in the history of the university, who had been president of the university boat club and played rugby for the university as a student, was a fierce upholder of the collegiate system and became in turn Censor, Bursar and eventually Master of University College: from 1922 he also coached the university boats and was chairman of the Durham regatta committee. Tim tried rowing but gave it up in preference to rugby and hockey, both of which he played for the college and hockey representatively for the Durham Colleges. Among his lecturers he was particularly interested by Professor F B Jevons, a pioneer in the sociology of religion, who lectured in Comparative Religion. Unfortunately, if Tim had an away match for the university hockey side he was unable to attend Jevons' lectures at 12 noon on Wednesdays and Saturdays. When he failed this course later, he felt that his absences had been noted and counted against him. Despite all this, Jevons had fired his interest in the subject, which was renewed as he met animism in Burma later; and he became an 'avid' reader of 'books on primitive religion in every part of the world'. Gowns were worn for lectures and in hall, as well as for any evening trips into the town.

Tim took a full part in the religious life of the University. He became president of the Evangelical Union, a precursor of the DICCU (Durham Inter-Collegiate Christian Union) and inherited a programme which included an open meeting to which the formidable bishop, Hensley Henson, was invited as speaker. Henson, no great admirer of evangelicals, Tim described well as 'diminutive', following the massive figure of the Dean, Bishop Welldon (an ex-metropolitan in India of Calcutta) in processions in the cathedral. Henson, however, though small, packed a punch as an orator and at this meeting, attended also by members of the high church college, St Chad's, took the opportunity to 'trounce Evangelicals' in a 'trenchant speech'. Tim, who had heard that Henson liked people to stand up to him, thanked the bishop for his 'scintillating rhetoric' and added that many present had not agreed with a word of it. He found Henson genial after this exchange: and himself received much 'popular support' for his riposte, not least from a member of St Chad's, who held that to respond to such an invitation as the bishop had done was 'a very unsporting thing', denigrating Evangelicals in a meeting open to all the university but set up by them. Tim wore his dog-collar round the university and this may have been the cause of the SCM asking him to lead a service to which Bishop Gore had been invited as speaker. He agreed but, in leading the bishop out when holding a large alms dish at the end of the service, he was unable to see that someone had put a litany desk in the aisle over which he nearly fell. On reaching the vestry, Bishop Gore asked 'what fool did that?', which Tim remembered better than Gore's address. Of other notables, he was able to entertain Bishop Howard Mowll as a speaker at a meeting specially arranged, before the bishop went out to Szechuan as an assistant in the diocese where Frank worked. Tim felt one man he knew may have heard a call to China at this meeting (he did serve in China) and that Mowll (later archbishop of Sydney) was 'very good'.

The year 1922 was very important to him. First, his engagement to Coralie was formalised on 31 July 1922, when she was aged 18 and he 26. Secondly, of very great importance for his future, was the formation of the BCMS on 27 October 1922. This had resulted from what many CMS supporters felt was a slide into liberalism in CMS. Led by Dr Daniel Bartlett a group of supporters made a conservative riposte, a group which included his father, as well as such leading evangelicals as Dean Wace and H E Fox, a former CMS secretary (G H G Hewitt, *Problems of Success: a history of the Church Missionary Society 1910-1942*, pp. 461-473 for a full account). In due course this was to open the way for his work among the Kachins, though at this stage both he and Coralie were potential candidates for the CIM in China. Coralie joined a CIM training college for women in Highbury for a two year course, funded by her parents, where she found the discipline strict and 'very irksome', one example being the requirement to wear both a blue uniform and matching bonnet: Tim was able to question this last requirement, his question was referred to the Ladies Council of CIM, who admitted that bonnets, in fashion when CIM was founded, had been required since then and not questioned but would now be dropped! CIM also had strict regulations over marriage and would not have countenanced Tim and Coralie marrying before going out to the field. This was one factor, and an important one, in a mutual sense of guidance towards BCMS, where Dr Bartlett, when consulted, saw no objection, a relief also to the Green parents who did not want their 18 year old daughter to go to China unaccompanied. Tim and Coralie were further encouraged by Tim's contacts among the American Baptists in Burma, who suggested that there was room for primary evangelism some 180 miles north of the Baptist mission at Shwebo, though it was to transpire later that Dr Hanson, a leading Baptist missionary, did not welcome the idea of an Anglican mission in this part of Burma and laid the issue before the Burma Christian Council. In December 1922, with all the future pending, Tim was priested in Rochester Cathedral, a much happier experience than his first ordination when he received a warm reception from Bishop Harmer, and retreat addresses from the Revd. Edward Lyttelton, once headmaster of Eton, whom Tim felt had 'something worth saying' and a good sense of humour in addition. He was pleased too, in the university, to win a university prize, the Long Reading prize and to be elected as president of the Castle Debating Union.

Tim spent the year following his curacy from October 1923 in study at the Missionary School of Medicine in Great Ormond Street, while boarding again at St John's, Highbury. Here he met again Roger Woodhams, who had been at Durham with him and had been the man most responsive to Bishop Howard Mowll; and also Marjorie Neill, whose parents had offered to serve with BCMS in India, where they were joined by Marjorie's brilliant young brother, Stephen Neill, Fellow of Trinity College, Cambridge acting as a lay missionary based at Dohnavur. Tim found Marjorie a 'lovely girl' but she was to die young of typhoid fever after joining her parents, by then working at Mirzapur. Tim, always aware of theological tendency, wrote of her brother that his 'views on the inspiration of the Bible were uncertain' but that 'later he did outstanding work in Tinnevelly before becoming bishop there', the admiration of one committed missionary for another. At MSM, in addition to some induction into general medicine and surgery, he learned enough of dentistry to be able to conduct extractions later in Burma and even to effect a self-extraction when troubled by an abscess with no anaesthetic and the judicious use of a mirror: he was proud not to break the tooth in the process.

By 1924 both Tim and Coralie were exercised about the future. Coralie had attended a missionary meeting addressed by J.O. Fraser, well known missionary of the Sino-Burma border, and through this had felt increasingly drawn to tribal work. Both looked towards the openings among the Kachins in Burma. Dr Bartlett, when consulted on the possibility, replied that BCMS might be willing to open a new field given suitable recruits. Two were immediately to hand. There were however hurdles to be overcome, the objections of the American Baptists, the hesitation of Bishop Fyffe of Rangoon, who until then had only SPG (Society for the Propagation of the Gospel) personnel in his care and was uncertain about another mission of a differing churchmanship. Tim pointed to his own knowledge of Burma through periods of domicile in 1916 and 1918, so being a 'veteran' of Burma rather than a novice and the bishop was reassured that finance would be found for them by the mission. A further 'hiccup' came when Bishop Cassels proposed Tim as a leader of a team of BCMS missionaries to serve in diocese of Szechuan, where Frank was working, a plan which found favour with Dr Bartlett and the BCMS staff as a leading from God. Tim and Coralie however still felt the call to Burma and the Kachins and felt that the emergence of BCMS and its willingness to open the field was of God. After an affirmative decision from the Bishop of Rangoon, BCMS finally agreed to send them; and their hesitations about Coralie's youth were allayed by Tim's sister Eileen, a qualified nurse, offering to go with them as an additional missionary.

On July 1st they were married at New Malden, with Bryan Green, now ordained, officiating and Thomas Houghton giving the address. His brother Stanley acted as his best man. The marriage was 'immediately followed by communion, as we had desired'. The honeymoon began in Boscastle but also included a week at High View, Limpley Stoke, where Aunt May had a tennis court for their entertainment on which they played daily. They spent time at Whitington Rectory and began to prepare for Burma. Rather to their dismay, Coralie showed early signs of pregnancy with 'morning sickness', so Burma would also mean childbirth and a family. They were able to plan for this by purchasing a folding pram before leaving, although their greatest reassurance must have rested in Eileen, who, as well as being a companion to Coralie, was a trained midwife to accompany them.

On September 30th 1924 Coralie celebrated her 20th birthday and during the month they attended a Valedictory Meeting arranged at Caxton Hall, which was shared among others with Roger Woodhams now bound for West China. Tim had his own valedictory moment in his father's church at Whitington, when it came to him with 'great force' that the call to which he had responded over many years was now 'an inevitable necessity'. He sang with a special depth of meaning 'We lose what on ourselves we spend, we have a treasure without end, whatever, Lord, to thee we lend, who givest all'. On October 10th they joined the Bibby line S.S. Oxfordshire and after a warm send-off from Birkenhead, which included two sons of Canon Wilkinson eager to see two 'real live missionaries', a description about which at this stage they felt uneasy, they sailed to Marseilles, Port Said, Colombo and finally Rangoon. It was the beginning of nearly twenty years of missionary service in Burma between 1925 to 1942.

CHAPTER 4

BCMS PIONEERS IN UPPER BURMA

Tim and Coralie's service in Burma falls fairly naturally into two periods, the first being between their arrival and their first furlough in England (1924-1929) and the second after their return to the now burgeoning mission until their final return to England (1930-1939). In his useful pamphlet *Burma – land of many tongues* (BCMS, 1948), Tim's colleague Wilfred Crittle described these contrasting eras. A work which had begun in 1924 with 'three agents of the society taking the gospel to Jinghpaws', seventeen years later was 'engaged in the task of helping with the evangelisation of at least twenty of the peoples', while the mission had grown from the original three to fifty missionaries on nineteen stations and four hospitals (p. 5).

On arrival in Rangoon on November 9, 1924, they were welcomed by the Port Chaplain and a friendly Indian doctor, who had instructions to convey them to Bishopscourt, the home of Bishop Fyffe. This was a relief, as they had nowhere to stay arranged beforehand. Tim had an appropriate quotation to hand from the martyr missionary Oliver Tompkins of New Guinea, a comment on John 21:4: 'Jesus stands on every shore to greet every missionary from every land', to which Tim added 'when he putteth forth his own sheep, he goeth before'. There were still delicate negotiations to navigate with the American Baptists and the Burma Christian Council if the Houghtons were to begin a pioneering mission among the Kachin people of the north. They travelled up the Irrawaddy to stay with a friendly ABM couple, Mr and Mrs Geis, who had been encouraging in correspondence, where the senior ABM missionary, Dr Hanson, had been opposed. Mr Geis remained warmly welcoming but felt bound by the Burma Council resolution, promoted by Dr Hanson. This prompted Tim to visit this senior figure in Bhamo personally. Although adhering to the resolution, Tim's visit reassured the Baptist sufficiently for Tim to write: 'the chief obstacle to starting work among the Kachins was removed', indeed Dr Hanson had 'thawed sufficiently to make it clear (that) he was really glad we might be working in the Hukawng Valley' and 'he was not surprised I wanted to work among the Kachins rather than among anyone else!'

The Kachins have attracted a number of modern studies by social anthropologists. They were animist in religion and their lives were dominated by spirits known as 'nats'. According to the *Encyclopedia of Religion* edited by Mircea Eliade (which contains an article 'nats') these were mainly ancestral spirits, who needed to be appeased and to whom offerings were made. Bamboo shrines to the nats were prevalent. Modern study has also shown that these hill peoples have two apparently contradictory forms of social organisation, a dependence on hierarchy (*gumsa*) and a more egalitarian social make-up (*gumlao*). The English anthropologist E.R. Leach, who, like Tim Houghton, gained his knowledge of Burma in large part as a British army officer, in his case in the 1939-45 war, wrote of the Kachins in *Political Systems of Highland Burma: a study of Kachin Social Structure* (1954), when he explained this variety in Kachin society, the place of the '*duwa*' or headman in groups of villages and the importance of *nats* in family life: 'every misfortune, illness, minor ailment or risky undertaking… is the occasion of a *masha nat* (ancestral spirit) sacrifice' (p. 110). It is interesting to notice that Leach listed two works by Dr Hanson among the sources for his study, a Kachin dictionary of 1906 and *The Kachins: their customs and traditions* of 1913.

Tim Houghton soon realised that, regardless of common custom and scholars' practice, because Kachin really meant 'savage' it was essential to call the people by their own preferred name of Jinghpaw, the basic meaning of which was 'man'. S.F. Russell, later a surgeon colleague in the mission, wrote of Tim's calling in his *Full Fifty Years* (1972): 'in December 1918, Captain A T Houghton could not foresee how God would call him to bring the gospel to the people of Burma's remote northern hills, Kachins, or as they call themselves, 'Jinghpaws' or men' (p. 14). It had happened, however, and Tim was to write a full and detailed account in his *Dense Jungle Green* (1937). Here the emphasis must be on his personal experience of the early period, when he and Coralie and Eileen were pioneers, Coralie aged 20 a very young missionary and mother-to-be.

Because the area of Upper Burma of his choice was in 'unadministered' territory, the Houghtons first had to get permission from the British authorities. After this they had to find somewhere to live. They decided to make the town of Mohnyin their base, a place 636 miles north of Rangoon and 60 miles west of the Irrawaddy, then the main thoroughfare to the south. From the start the aim was a strictly evangelistic mission, unencumbered by institutions, reaching the often neglected hill tribes, where much effort concentrated on the towns. Tim was wary of missions which became heavily institutionalised by over emphasis, for example, on schools. In the foreword to *Dense Jungle Green* Admiral Sir Harry Stileman wrote: 'the method of pioneer evangelism in contradistinction to excessive institutionalism is the plan upon which this mission has worked: every missionary first and foremost an evangelist' (p. 7): of this he had direct knowledge through his own daughter, M F (May) Stileman, who was among the earliest recruits in 1926, later assigned to Bilumyo among the Shan people.

After a temporary stay in a vacant police bungalow, where they were helped to settle by the friendly wife of a District Officer, Mrs Dewar, the same friend was instrumental in finding a more permanent home for them in Mohnyin in a bungalow no longer required by the commercial firm Steele Brothers. Tim Houghton wrote of their arrival here on December 18th, 1924 that 'ever since (that) has been regarded as the day on which the Burma mission was founded'. To reach it they needed steady nerves. The only route was 'a tumbledown suspension bridge', consisting of one or two planks forty foot above the stream. This had no handrail and tipped at 'alarming angles' a high test for his pregnant wife, whose foot went through a wooden hole on her way across. The dwelling which greeted them was enough to depress the spirits of the most intrepid pioneers, grimy, covered in smoke and full of cobwebs, overseen by a Burmese caretaker who 'being consumptive…coughed and spat alternatively'. A large hole in the walls was matched by chickens in what purported to be the bathroom.

The one visual encouragement was a beautiful flowering bougainvillea: 'somehow,' he wrote, 'that made all the difference'.

Despite enduring great frustrations with the contractor and his carpenters, they moved in and even began Sunday services on their verandah, attended by some twenty local people. They had three Kachin servants, Ma Tang the cook, Ma Yaw for household duties and Ma Naw as water carrier and gardener: all came to the Sunday service and were quick to grasp the idea of no work on Sundays. A temporary dispensary for Eileen was established in the servants' quarters of the house and the first patient was treated on January 1st 1925, a baby suffering from diarrhoea and vomiting who was cured. The father, a Sikh, brought presents in gratitude and news of the cure spread. This in turn led to the need for a regular dispensary with set opening hours. This medical work did wonders for breaking down initial suspicions, though they found that rather than the Jinghpaws, whose language they were slowly learning, the patients were Shans, Burmese, Indians and Chinese. On home visits, they were accompanied by the sympathetic (though Muslim) contractor, acting as interpreter, who pleased Tim by referring to his role as 'Assistant to Lord Jesus', 'an office we greatly longed to fulfil'.

He was about to become a father. Timothy Patrick, known as Pat was born at 11.35pm on Saturday 25 January 1925, with Eileen acting as midwife. At the delivery, Coralie sang in her best Jinghpaw 'Rai sa, tsaw ra ai' (Yes, Jesus loves me). A son greatly delighted the local Jinghpaw, whom they named Zau Gam, Zau being the title given to the son of a chief, while Gam indicated firstborn. Pat was the apple of his father's eye, who 'never imagined I should be so interested in a baby'. At the birth they had been plagued by flying ants. Now, the grass roof, subjected to torrential rainstorms, began to leak and then to 'rain' snakes. Faced with a new roof to install and an annexe to build for the new missionary recruits before their arrival in the autumn, Coralie, Tim, Eileen and the baby were ready to move out for a holiday after Pat's baptism on June 21st. Eileen described their next alarming experience on a bullock cart fording a river: 'the bullocks were soon out of their depth and with a rush the water swept right over the cart where we were sitting...I got up...and held Baby aloft and Coralie, still keeping a Burmese umbrella over his head, seized Tim's attaché case and we just clung on and laughed at the strange experience'.

After the holiday they tried to establish a daily pattern, rising at 6am, with Jinghpaw prayers at 7.30, dispensary at 7.40 – 10 when they had breakfast, followed by English prayers at 10.45, language study from 11 – 1pm, rest, tea, more language study (2.30 – 4.15), exercise (4.15 – 5.15), dinner at 6.45 and evening prayers at 8.30. This basic pattern was upset both by Tim's illness with dengue fever and such interruptions as the Diocesan Council in Rangoon. For this, Tim stayed with a Colonel Middleton-West, a member of the Officers' Christian Union and Civil Surgeon in Rangoon General Hospital, driven in the surgeon's motor car by a long-serving SPG missionary, George West, who became bishop of Rangoon later. Tim found his fellow clergy, whether SPG missionaries or diocesan chaplains, very friendly: he was identified by Bishop Fyffe as a pioneer, living 'in the back of beyond'. As will appear, Tim made a consistent contribution to diocesan affairs, at considerable personal cost in terms of travel (600 miles) and as a lone voice from a different tradition on such as the debate over the 1927/8 revised prayer book. His courage in debate earned him only the respect and admiration of his fellow clergy. Bishop Fyffe made a personal visit to their bungalow in August, which by then to their relief had a serviceable teak shingle roof. BCMS had approved the annexe for the new recruits at a cost of £375 and had increased their salary from £250 to £300: 'we had never grumbled but we had informed Dr Bartlett of the financial situation, so were very grateful', for, he wrote. 'we had often been down to our last penny'.

They were surprised to hear in October that the new recruits had already sailed and were due in Rangoon on November 3rd. This resulted in an ultimatum to the contractor towards the completion of the annexe for Wilfred Crittle and Vera Perry to be accommodated. There were growing anxieties about Eileen Houghton's health, at a time when they added to their establishment by acquiring two important animals: Daniel, a pony, who was to carry Tim for 'hundreds of miles over hill and plain' and a wire haired fox terrier called Tiger. Daniel's legs had effectively been 'auctioned' by Coralie's father, which raised the 65 rupees needed to buy him. On arrival, Wilfred Crittle and Vera Perry, aged 21 and 25, threw themselves into language study with enthusiasm, though, with the annexe still not completed, Tim's study had to be surrendered to Crittle and Miss Perry had to share a bedroom with Eileen.

As the first year in the field ended, Tim's mind was exploring moves into Hukawng Valley and towards the Naga hills, home to head hunting tribes who were known also to practice human sacrifice. A day of prayer and conference was set apart on November 23rd to consider missionary strategy, which resulted in an appeal to BCMS for four more workers for the Shans and four for the Burmese, adding to the main thrust towards the Kachins. Eileen had given herself to the study of the Burmese language but in December medical opinion decreed that she must go home to recover from a heart condition and only return if recovery was complete. This was a considerable blow to the infant mission and its medical provision. She sailed home in March 1926, by which time Wilfred Crittle and Vera Perry were unofficially engaged. A new bungalow had been approved in a healthy setting 2,500 feet above sea level at Hkapra as a refuge from the hot weather and the dangers to health that it brought. Pat's first bout of malaria drove home the lesson that few escaped the disease in their first rainy season.

The mission was reinforced in 1926 by the arrival of May Stileman, Admiral Stileman's daughter, with two ordained men in Ted Rushton and Albert Fowler and two other workers in Elizabeth Lane and Doris Harris. A welcome missionary visitor was Tim's brother Stanley, on his way to China and the CIM and godfather to Pat. Tim had heard from China of the deaths in quick succession of Bishop and Mrs Cassels, a source of deep sorrow to Frank and his wife Dorrie, their daughter, in Paoning, though Stanley's initial destination was to be Shanghai. During his stay Stanley left a vivid account of his journey by pony from Mohnyin, 600 feet above sea level, to Hkapra (and above) where they reached 3,750 feet: he and others had a miraculous escape from injury when a pack pony stampeded from the tops, frightening the other ponies and delivering all the contents of their panniers (including medicines, a concertina and their provisions) all over the mountain, littering the ground and requiring extensive re-packing. It was an illustration of the essential nature of the ponies for travel but also the perils they could constitute. Tim, on the basis of his experience in Bangalore in1918, became riding master for the others, who had to master this essential skill for transport in the hills. Before Stanley left them, the mission had a letter from Dr Hanson of ABM with 'the glorious news that he had finished translating the whole Bible (into Kachin)': 'can you imagine how thrilling it is' Tim wrote to England 'the *whole* of the

Word of God for the first time in Kachin!' It was an asset beyond compare for both mission and church.

In 1927 Tim gave considerable attention to village evangelism. Once more this involved ponies, two of whom carried his tent, valise, camp bed and table, magic lantern, kerosene oil and provisions. When he could he slept in Kachin houses: though like many missionaries, which viewers of the film *The Piano* will remember was the experience among the Maori, Jinghpaws denied all privacy, making such activities as the preparation of addresses difficult. Long discussions could result from these talks in homes, with one saying 'we ought to know more about God' and another 'yes, we must worship him', only to be answered 'we shall have to give up the *nats* then', followed by an influential woman saying 'no, we must *not* give up the *nats*', in what Tim noted was 'a rather angry tone'. A headman of the village proved very friendly and invited a further visit: Tim had discussions with his daughter, who had acted as *ayah* (nurse) for them, and found that she was 'genuinely converted', one sign of which was a new courage in the dark: her previous deep fear of *nats* and tigers had gone. She told Tim 'with a bright smile' 'Duwa, if we believe in Jesus, we shall go to be with him in heaven, shan't we?' Tim found a group of boys in a village six miles from Hkapra, one of whom had learned choruses at the mission, which made him seriously consider a small primary school for them, despite his hesitations over schools and institutions. He wrote of these opportunities in the hills: 'it was a privilege to tell them something of the Lord Jesus. These isolated opportunities are very solemn responsibilities, for one feels that in preaching to these people the Kingdom of God has come nigh to them'.

Evangelism led to baptisms. Early in July 1927 Tim recorded the first Jinghpaw baptisms 'the great event of the month towards which we had been eagerly looking forward'. To ensure that there was no obvious rift in practice between themselves and the Baptist ABM mission, the form used was baptism by immersion. A congregation of 50 stood at the riverside, matched on the other bank by 100-150 Shans and Burmese. The two to be baptised were Ma Yaw and Ma Kaw, the first a member of their household, who had sought their approval of Ma Kaw as his wife: after serving as Pat's *ayah* she received Christ in April 1927 and became 'approved' for him. Ma Yaw, who had renounced both opium and strong drink, now gave evidence at the riverside of his freedom from the *nats* and his trust in the cross of

Christ. Tim wrote in *Dense Jungle Green* that 'indescribable thrill came over me as I baptised Ma Yaw and Ma Kaw into the Triune name' and in his letter to England 'needless to say my heart was too full for words – the nucleus of the Jinghpaw church in Mohnyin....has begun'.

Another individual conversion led to him writing a small book called *Tailum Jan* published in 1930. It is a vivid and accessible account of a Jinghpaw widow, born Ma Roi but wife of Tailum (so Tailum Jan), whose husband had died after twelve years of married life. As a widow she had few, if any, rights, becoming the property of her late husband's relations. On one of Tim Houghton's village visits she attended to the message about the lost sheep: she prayed with him 'I want a clean heart' (p. 35). Her conversion was real but was tested by an encounter with an angry bear. In slashing the undergrowth with her *dah*, she wounded the prostrate animal, who pinned her to the ground. Her companions fled, thinking her doomed. Death was imminent but she prayed an arrow prayer 'Karai Kasang e, ngai hpe karum e law' ('O God, Help me'). The bear 'rose and unsteadily wobbled off', leaving her mauled and bleeding but, to the amazement of others with experience of bears, still alive. Although she faced formidable opposition from her 'owner', Tailum La, the relation who laid claim to her, she was baptised by Tim Houghton, whom she knew as 'Du Kaba', the Big Chief. This simply told story of 114 pages, able to be appreciated by any reader or supporter of missions young or old, displayed some of the same skill in popular communication of that doyen of such literature in Germany of the 1920s, Christian Keysser, missionary to savage tribes of New Guinea between 1901-1920. In due course Tailum Jan was confirmed by the bishop in the first such service ever held in Mohnyin, in a group which also contained a Jinghpaw son of a murderer who had been hanged.

The years of 1927 and1928 had presented a severe personal crisis to Tim Houghton, as also his father at home. The Church of England was in the process of providing a revised prayer book, by which the bishops hoped to end disputes about what were permissible uses. In order to accommodate Anglo-Catholics certain concessions had been made on such matters as reservation of the consecrated elements for Holy Communion, prayers for the dead, vestments and a version of the prayer of consecration which deeply offended many evangelicals.

Tailum Jan – an early Jinghpaw convert
who had an encounter with an angry bear

Tim's father was among those most vigorously opposed to these changes, believing that in the 1662 book, based on the work of Thomas Cranmer, they had a guarantee of scripturally sound, Reformed worship: to depart from it would mean that their position as evangelicals in the Church of England would no longer be tenable. At the diocesan discussions in Rangoon, Tim himself had earned plaudits from those of different views, by speaking courteously but firmly of evangelical objections to the new book: he admitted to hating controversy and spoke very reluctantly but his interventions, which required much courage, resulted in 'a quite unexpected round of applause, specially from the laity' and all 'gave me a splendid hearing' a number of the clergy who took the other side going out of their way to thank him for his main speech.

Leaving the Church of England was a matter of deep and grave concern to him, combined with the anxiety of what would happen to his parents who would be deprived of their living and home. It is easy to imagine his intense relief and sheer delight when, against all expectation, the revised book was successfully opposed in parliament in a debate where Sir William Joynson-Hicks led the opposition. Tim had written gloomily before this event: 'the Ecclesiastical Committee (of parliament) has responded favourably to Parliament on the Deposited Book...it made me feel the severity of the issue as never before, for it may be that very soon we shall be called upon to make the actual personal decision'. Then, on December 23rd he wrote in a letter: 'everything else is overshadowed by the glorious news of the rejection of the Prayer Book Measure by the House of Commons. What hath God wrought! The news was almost too overwhelming'. His sense of extreme relief is all too clear, an indication of his deep loyalty to the Church of England but also of a readiness to override this on principle, even if very unwillingly.

Before he and Coralie left for their furlough in February 1929 there were various developments as the mission grew. After a conference of their own it was agreed that there should be an advisory committee to assist Tim in his work as superintendent. He commented that he had no desire for power and was happy for others to share it: but while 'I have no *desire* for power...it is essential that a superintendent should superintend'. Nevertheless, he refused to inhibit the wishes of other missionaries, subject only to sanction by the Home Committee. Ecclesiastically, Bishop Fyffe was succeeded by Bishop Tubbs, with whom Tim developed a warm relationship. Tubbs had come from South India and greatly admired the work of Amy Carmichael at Dohnavur and the prayerful approach of her mission. Tim found that the bishop had attended Keswick, had a background of the Christian Union (CICCU) at Cambridge as well as a soccer blue and showed himself no stranger to extempore prayer when praying with Tim for his work. He had been the confirming bishop for Tailum Jan at Mohnyin where 'the converts listened with rapt attention and were greatly delighted that in confirming the Bishop was able to use their own Jinghpaw language'. Tim was also cheered by news that the newly appointed governor, Sir Charles Innes, was likely to prove supportive to his plans for a pioneering mission in the north. This suggestion was welcome: 'His Excellency....said he thought he could say definitely that provided we would undertake to begin a *medical* mission work in the Hukawng Valley, no opposition would be raised on the part of the Government', which may have indicated that government saw humanitarian relief as a way of pacifying the fierce hill tribes like the Nagas. Tim was content: 'we shall not be allowed to go into the human sacrificing area and our own area will be 'delimited' but the great thing is that the way will now be open. Hallelujah!' The news brought home their need for a doctor, a need which he took home with him on furlough.

The growth of the mission to nearly twenty workers (listed in Appendix 'D' of Hooton and Wright's history of the BCMS at p. 228) opened them to fresh language groups. May Stileman and Doris Harris had studied Burmese since 1926, a means of reaching the Shan people, and this focus was shared by Doris Parker, Lilian Mason, Gertie Sagar and Adelaide Sharpe, who was the first nurse to arrive after Eileen Houghton's departure, and who took charge of the dispensary at Mohnyin. Now a further dispensary was opened in Bilumyo, west of Mohnyin, where in time 70-80 patients per day were treated and the medical provision was shared between Misses Stileman and Dorothy Bond. The move to the north and Hukawng Valley led to a station being opened at Indaw, which had both a Shan population and gave access to the Kadu people who numbered around 37,000 and their near kin the Gaman, who numbered 7,000 at the time. Here the Revd. Harold Kitchen and his bride settled in 1929. A development of quite a different kind was the invitation to the mission to take over a Deaf and Dumb institution, as it was then called, known as the Mary Chapman Training College in Rangoon. Miss Chapman had served with CEZMS (Church of England Zenana Missionary Society) in India and at the age of 60 wanted to hand this work in Burma to the BCMS. Tim became aware of its significance on a personal visit, both as a means of reaching the many deaf children of Burma and as a base for the mission's activities in Rangoon. He wrote later that, unknown to him at the time, this development was almost as momentous for the future as the governor's agreement to proceed north 'though I little realised it then'. It was to provide an essential head-quarters as the mission's responsibilities spread and grew, a site of great strategic importance for the future of the mission.

Before they left Burma, Coralie was ill with a 'very bad bout of malaria' and, for the first time, Tim himself was very seriously ill with what was diagnosed as typhoid but he believed to be malignant malaria. He believed that intra muscular injections given him by an Indian doctor in Mandalay saved his life and a second quinine injection finally brought his temperature under control: 'I have never been so really *ill* in my life and praise God for his goodness in bringing me safely through'. He was able to leave the mission in the hands of Wilfred (Bill) Crittle, by now married to Vera Perry, and they sailed from Rangoon with Pat and their second child, Betty (baptised Elizabeth Coralie), whose first birthday they celebrated on board on February 17th and for whom a birthday cake was provided. He wrote in *Dense Jungle Green* that it was an opportunity both for recuperation from an exhausting and debilitating tour of service and time for reflection: like moving in the jungle 'an occasional glimpse of mountain and plain from a clearing at the top gives one an unexpected view, which enables one to see the whole in right perspective. Furlough tends to have the same useful effect…the tendency is to lose the wider vision. It is a good thing to be able to get right away for a season, and in communion with God to seek and obtain inspiration for the future'. So ended the first and pioneering phase of their service.

CHAPTER 5

BURMA: DEVELOPMENTS IN MISSION AND CHURCH

On the first furlough the special needs of the mission were the cause of much prayer and reflection. As a base, Tim and Coralie were offered space in Coralie's parents' home in New Malden, where Bryan Green and his new wife, Win, occupied a lower flat. It was a time when Frank, invalided home from China and working as editorial secretary of the CIM, was also in the London area. If BCMS were to take up the opening in the Hukawng Valley, offered by Sir Charles Innes, there was need for qualified medical personnel. It was a huge relief to Tim when Colonel Middleton-West, after retiring to Bristol after years of work in Burma as a Civil Surgeon, offered with his wife to return to Burma with BCMS to work in the Hukawng Valley. Here was a medical professional already very highly regarded throughout Burma, with whom Tim had stayed in Rangoon for a diocesan conference after recommendations of him as a member of the Officers' Christian Union and whom he had come to respect and trust. Stanley Farrant Russell, a highly skilled young surgeon, also offered for the work and reached Burma with his wife in 1930.

If the medical side could be resolved, Tim Houghton was still left with the serious issue of the increasingly burdensome accounting and business administration of the growing BCMS work, which had begun to weigh on him heavily as someone, for example, with no training in accountancy. It came as a great encouragement that another middle-aged couple in

Mr and Mrs Hubert Green, Coralie's parents and in her father's case a member of the BCMS executive, proved willing to live in the so-called Deaf and Dumb institution, given to BCMS by Miss Chapman, with Hubert Green taking over the business administration and its burdens. To Tim Houghton this was 'a glorious answer to prayer'. The Greens were to serve for five years (1930-35), during which Mrs Green extended much care to the deaf children and her husband gave invaluable aid in running the growing mission from this base in Rangoon.

The other hope had been to recruit further ordained men for the mission. Here Tim felt that he was taught a salutary lesson about whom to take into his confidence. During his many deputation engagements while on furlough was a visit to a church in Weymouth, where he stayed with a hospitable clergy family called Lankester, the vicar being a member of the BCMS executive. Here he met Stafford Wright, the curate, who had expressed interest in BCMS work in Burma when an undergraduate in Cambridge, where he had been a scholar of Sidney Sussex College. When Tim Houghton explained the needs, Stafford Wright expressed willingness to serve in Burma in the following autumn if he could be released from his curacy. Tim, eager to be transparent, told Lankester of this: but no sooner had Lankester seen him off, than he took the first train to London, insisted on an interview with Dr Bartlett and extracted a promise that he would not lose his curate to BCMS. Tim later found Bartlett adamant that, despite Stafford Wright's willingness to serve, BCMS would not permit the plan. In the end, Stafford Wright never served abroad but he gave sterling service to BCMS as a theological teacher, being in turn a lecturer and vice-principal of Tyndale Hall (1930-37, 1937-45), before becoming its principal between 1951 -1969. He was also co-author of the early history of BCMS with W S Hooton, *The First Twenty-Five Years* (BCMS, 1947). Among many other deputation engagements, Tim visited Dublin, where he met Hugh Jordan, later principal of the London College of Divinity and then curate at St Kevin's, Dublin and renewed his friendship with Martin Parsons, then secretary of the CMS Hibernian Society, who had been converted in the Tunbridge Wells mission of January 1922. Tim was also glad to be given five minutes to explain BCMS work in Burma at the Keswick Convention's big missionary meeting in the summer.

Their return to Burma coincided with two events which caught the attention of the world press. As they arrived by sea in 1930 Amy

Johnson, the aviatrix who made a solo flight to Australia as a woman pilot, flew over Akyab and touched down at Rangoon. Secondly, the Simon report on British administration in India and Burma was published and recommended the administrative division of Burma from India, a policy that Tim heartily endorsed. The mission's long awaited entry into the Hukawng Valley took place, an area well described by Tim Houghton in *Dense Jungle Green* (p. 148ff.): 'the snow capped mountains of southern Tibet effectually enclose the valley on the north; while in the west is the Patkoi range, which divides Burma from Assam and is inhabited on both sides by various tribes of Nagas'. Colonel Middleton-West led the mission which arrived on March 6, 1930, assisted by Dr. S.F. Russell and, later, by Dr. W.B. Johnston and his wife who, as Miss Collyer, had nursed at the little hospital from 1932. They were confronted by much opium addiction among many flourishing poppy fields, considerable lawlessness and many vendettas, which inculcated much fear in the local population. The medical mission made steady progress, treating many from the surrounding villages and resulting also in the first Hukawng Valley baptism by Tim on an evangelistic tour in 1931-2 of Ma Tawng; and, more directly from their medical work, the baptism of a woman leper, Ma Hatu, in October 1933, recorded by Tim in *Dense Jungle Green* (pp. 158-9). By then BCMS had acquired an elephant, named Maggie (*magwi* being the Jinghpaw name for elephant) who tramped through the Hukawng Valley shifting logs and delivering mail in the rainy season.

In addition to the Hukawng Valley, plans had been laid to gain access to the very different area of the Arakan, low lying land bordering the Bay of Bengal with Akyab as its chief centre. Here Tim discovered that waterways were the means of travel but not before he had attempted an exhausting overland journey into Chin country which 'proved to be the most strenuous (march) ever taken'. An independent Welsh missionary called Rowlands had worked in the north of the Arakan. Tim got to his base at Paletwa. He found that Rowlands was using Lushai evangelists and had also married a Lushai wife but wanted now to hand over the work to BCMS. Harold Hacking, the BCMS missionary then working in Akyab and serving the expatriate church there at the Bishop of Rangoon's request, accompanied Tim on the Chin expedition, where the going was so hard that they covered four and a half miles in eight hours: having risen at 4.30am, they were both so exhausted by 1pm that they were unable to continue. There is no doubt that Tim enjoyed these adventurous journeys, despite their demands: he wrote in *Dense Jungle Green*: 'there is nothing more physically exhilarating than going off the beaten track, where white men are hardly known, with the purpose of discovering new territory and preparing the way for the proclamation of the gospel. Such adventures have been some of the most enjoyable experiences in breaking new ground for pioneer missionary work' (p. 201). He gave vivid descriptions of journeys by dugout canoe, both to reach Paletwa in 1932 (pp. 179-183) and also through the rapids of the Chindwin river from Dalu in the far north (pp. 203-210), an attempt to see if direct communication between the Dalu Valley and the Jade mines area further south was possible, an occasion when he encountered Naga fishermen with thousands of dead fish drying in the sun and persuaded his companions to move on rather than spend the night inhaling the stench of the huge catch. Whether on foot, by pony (his pony Daniel travelled hundreds of miles) or by dugout canoe the journey was physically demanding and dangerous, as was illustrated by Hacking swimming the river but the crew of a steamer warning Tim that a crocodile had devoured a woman there three days earlier. Tim accepted the dissuasive and Hacking survived to become Field Secretary of the Arakan mission in the later 1930's.

Various other initiatives were taken. One missionary became aware of 300,000 Bengali Muslims in the Arakan area: Ernest Francis, who arrived in 1932, devoted his ministry to them. The area of the Jade Mines provided a further challenge, the jade having for centuries been highly prized in China, where it had often been transported by mules for generations. The BCMS couple, the Rushtons, established a mission based at Lonkin to reach this area, which was well north of the main BCMS station at Mohnyin, and they were assisted by a committed national in Hkamaw Gam, preacher, teacher of reading to Christians and dispenser of medicine. Further south, at Wuntho, work was begun among 9,000 Burmese by two BCMS women missionaries, Misses Harris and McKellen, in what was known as a stronghold of Buddhism and highly resistant to their work. In assessing the response of the different races in *Dense Jungle Green* in 1936, Tim Houghton could list Jinghpaws (and associated Kachin groups) at 256 but only 29 Burmese to match them (p. 29).

During this second period of service, Tim recorded a number of 'firsts': at Bilumyo there was the baptism of the first convert, Maung Aw, in February 1932, followed by the first Shan converts in May 1934. These

49

Shans had been preceded however by a Shan 'princess' from over the border in China, Nang Bao Gyin, who had learned of Christ during visits to her relations in Bilumyo. She obtained the permission of her husband, ruler (*sawbwa*) of the Shan state over the border, to be baptised. An event that Tim regarded as of special significance for the future of the church in Burma was the first ordination of a national on May 3, 1936: U Set Paw was a Karen teacher from a Christian (ABM) background, who had been much troubled by working in a school which only observed Buddhist holidays and required him to work on Sundays. This led, after much heart-searching over a long period, to resignation, at which point he was offered work at a lower salary by the mission. His ordination as deacon was a matter of joy to Tim: mission, he wrote, was not only about converts but also ministers: 'such indigenous ministers of the Gospel are essential to the building up of the Body of Christ (Eph. 4:12) if the visible church... is to grow in a healthy and normal way'.

Along with these causes of thanksgiving went experiences of loss. Adelaide Sharpe, a missionary nurse, as we have seen earlier arrived in Burma in November 1928, filling the gap left by Eileen Houghton's enforced return home. As the medical staff was strengthened in 1930 she contracted bacillary dysentery, and, although nursed day and night and in the expert care of Colonel Middleton-West, she died in September 1930. She had feared dying without fruit from her mission. It was not until three years later that another missionary discovered a woman in one of the nearby villages who had come to faith through her service, while another woman, antagonistic to her husband's Christian profession as a believing Burmese, duly sought baptism and explained 'ever since Miss Sharpe's death she had longed to repent, for she realised that Miss Sharpe had laid down her life to bring the knowledge of Jesus to such as her' (*Dense Jungle Green*, p. 142). S F Russell's wife died in 1932 as did the missionary Doris Parker after seven years work among the Shan. There were also deaths of early Christian converts, Ma Roi (about whom Tim had written in *Tailum Jan*) in 1930 and Ma Yaw, first Chin convert of the mission, in 1937. These losses were balanced by Set Paw being ordained priest in March 1937 along with the first Jinghpaw ordinand, Hkamaw Gam, ordained deacon in the same service.

Ordinations and confirmations were not the only basis for Tim holding, contrary to his father's views, that bishops were of the *bene esse* (for the good) of the church's life. He held them to be important in the leadership of both mission and church. His own relationships with successive bishops in Fyffe and Tubbs and West were uniformly good and of encouragement to him, as was his relationship to Foss Westcott, the seventy-five year old metropolitan, who paid a ten yearly visit on behalf of CIPBC (the Church of India, Pakistan, Burma and Ceylon) in 1934: Tim wrote of his great admiration for the elderly bishop's simplicity of life and willingness to endure hardness during his visit. When Bishop Tubbs resigned in 1934, he strongly commended to Tim Houghton Stephen Neill's name as a potential successor, Neill then being at work in the Tinnevelly diocese. Tim knew Marjorie Neill had been anxious about her brother's theological position as tending towards liberalism and he also knew that there had been differences with the great evangelical figure Amy Carmichael of Dohnavur, where Neill had lived (on Bishop Tubbs' account, Tubbs when still in Tinnevelly found Neill a teaching job when Neill was no longer welcome in Dohnavur). Despite any doubts this may have raised, Tim voted for Neill, who did indeed come first of four candidates, but pleaded to be excused on psychological grounds. George West, the next candidate listed, was a SPG missionary who had been influenced by MRA (Moral Rearmament) and the Oxford Groups of the time, a man Tim admired and found very open in relationships, the one *caveat* being his views on guidance, a source of difficulty when the guidance changed and the positions previously adopted with it. West was consecrated Bishop of Rangoon on January 25, 1935.

A diocesan conference of July 1936 considered the future of the diocese. Although later a new diocese of Mandalay began to be canvassed for the north, at this stage there was the interim suggestion of an assistant bishop. Tim himself was asked to move a resolution towards this to a Diocesan Council on July 30th without knowing that this was to have far-reaching effects on his own life, when the bishop asked him to fill the role in a letter of April 29, 1939. Initially, this suggestion came as a considerable shock and even as an unwelcome interruption of his and Coralie's intentions of further service in the growing BCMS mission in the north. In July 1938 the proposal for the eventual formation of a new diocese of Mandalay had been moved and accepted. In his speech on the proposal, the Revd. W R Garrad, a SPG missionary admired by Tim in general and for his scholarly expositions of the Bible, had said: 'to an outsider it might appear as if differences of churchmanship have become the reasons for the separations. But to those who know the diocese and the happy relationship between the BCMS and SPG such is not at all the case; and, as someone remarked when we were leaving the hall, a society which puts the Bible first in its name cannot be very far removed from a society which ends up with the gospel'. Tim Houghton himself spoke in this debate and was reported in the *Church Times*, emphasising that the proposed division did not imply separation and that, during the session of the council which considered the issue, he himself had realised a new conception of the catholic church.

Meanwhile, family affairs had developed. Rachel Mary had been born in 1929 (20 October 1929) to add to Pat and Betty. In 1934 Monica Joan was added to the family (8 June 1934). Tim's sister Freda offered to CIM and went to China, meaning that four out of the eight children of his generation became missionaries. It prompted him to write to his parents: 'it is wonderful news but I know it will not be easy…to give up another to the Lord for his work abroad but you have never held back your dearest from him and he will make it up in giving you joy in the sacrifice'. Sadly, Freda died early in her service in China in 1932 from meningitis, one year after her arrival. Tim's mother died in 1934 and he noted that the day of her death was the same date (July 3rd) that Herbert had been lost on the Somme. Frank, now fit for overseas service, was appointed Bishop of East Szechwan and consecrated in January 1937. Beryl Margaret's birth (8 February 1936) was followed by Michael's birth in 1938 (3 November 1938) as Michael Bryan Brockwell which completed Tim and Coralie's family of two boys and four girls, which he described to supporters in a letter as a 'quiverful'. As parents on furlough in the mid-1930's they had felt keenly the decision to leave Pat, aged 10½, at Monkton Combe Junior School. Tim knew the headmaster, the Revd. Edward Hayward, from the past and was introduced on a visit to the head boy, Maurice (M A P) Wood, son of the evangelist Arthur Wood and in due course Bishop of Norwich. He wrote of this separation: 'never before have we felt so much the cost of responding to God's call'. It was a searching decision faced by many missionaries in the interests of their children's education. Pat, whatever his first reactions, seems to have flourished in the school, was second in his form order and captain of the preparatory school's rugby team, in due course sitting a scholarship for the senior school. His parents kept his photograph prominently in their missionary living room and chose two Biblical texts to put under it, Coralie's being Hebrews 5:8: 'though he was a son, yet he learned obedience by the things which he suffered'. This and

Tim's choice of 'I know whom I have believed' had a prominent place in their home in Mohnyin for four years.

Tim faced difficulties with BCMS headquarters and in particular with Dr Bartlett, of whom, as founding father of BCMS, there is a helpful memoir by G W Bromiley, *Daniel Henry Charles Bartlett MA, DD: a memoir* (1959). He had firmly supported the Houghtons in their early days as we have seen, both personally and financially when need arose. Tim was aware of his polemical attitudes, which had been the cause of alienating some from the society, but his own relationship with him had been good. By now, however, he wrote of Bartlett: 'there were already the seeds of megalomania which showed itself in his attitude towards the executive committee where he ensured that he had his own way'. As Tim saw it, allies at the heart of BCMS like Dame Violet Wills and the treasurer, S H Gladstone, who gave the secretary their unquestioning support, only served to compound the problem of authoritative direction. Tim had already discovered that, on the kind of policy questions raised by the writings, for example, of Roland Allen, on missionary strategy and the indigenous church, Dr Bartlett was not a source for advice: 'I had tried to get from Dr Bartlett some indication of missionary policy' he wrote '(but) I got no help at all and soon realised that he had not a clue what policy should be pursued beyond the preaching of the gospel'.

Now a serious difference of opinion arose over the purchase of a school for the education of the children of the missionaries. The Misses Cousins had offered to BCMS for this work and in addition had given a donation of £1,000 towards it in 1933. The society was prepared to give £10,000 for the purchase of a school building. In 1934 the Cousins found Woodlands at Kalaw, regarded as an ideal site but costing £15,000. Generously the sisters offered to find the extra £5,000 themselves. To Tim's dismay, Dr Bartlett refused to countenance the purchase of any building beyond the £10,000 limit, even though the society would not pay more than this under the plan proposed. Tim wrote: 'It seemed as if we were absolutely stuck, for the first time I absolutely rebelled against such an unreasonable decision'. Cables and letters went back and forth and eventually Tim tried to circumvent Dr Bartlett's intransigence by appealing directly to members of the BCMS executive, asking the committee to override the secretary, a move he later regretted and one which he felt cast him in the role of a rebellious superintendent from Burma. The crisis was eventually resolved by the Cousins sisters paying the whole purchase price after recovering their £1,000 from BCMS.

When new structures of missionary government were proposed from home, 'superintendents' became secretaries to Field Councils in October 1934. Although he revealed none of his feelings in *Dense Jungle Green* (p. 213), Tim felt that, in part, this was a riposte 'probably a direct result of my action, the decision was reached to take away the power exercised up to now of superintendents with sole authority in the various fields'. Amicable correspondence with headquarters was resumed but Tim was aware that 'behind it was a determination to keep me in my place'. When Mr and Mrs Hubert Green reached the end of their five year contract with BCMS it is plain that Tim had hoped for some flexibility to extend the assistance they had given to the mission from Rangoon. He found however that Dr Bartlett was 'adamant' that there would be no extension: he wrote 'I was aware that having blotted my copybook on the house at Kalaw…my plans might be thwarted', as indeed they were. Nevertheless, when confronted by Bishop West's invitation to serve the diocese in an episcopal role, Tim found both Dr Bartlett and the BCMS executive uniformly sympathetic and willing for him to remain an honorary missionary of the society when a bishop, reluctant as they must have been to lose him as a missionary leader in their work: their attitude, and that of the Burma mission, that it was a clear call from God, reassured him in his response. Dr Bartlett's cable of 26 May 1939 to them both read: 'regretfully but sympathetically agree go forward with all your proposals retain you honorary missionaries'. Tim had aired his doubts to the bishop, including those of integrity in regard to churchmanship and communion practice, but in a letter of May 12, 1939 he wrote; 'I have no shadow of doubt now that I am meant to accept the call and go forward step by step as God guides'.

Tim and Coralie sailed on the SS Oronsay and arrived into Plymouth Sound on July 26, 1939, little realising that this was to prove the conclusion of their fifteen years of service in Burma, let alone that in a matter of weeks war would be declared with Germany in September. Nevertheless, at this stage, the *Times* of 21 March 1940 announced that 'the Bishop of Rangoon, with the approval of the Metropolitan of Calcutta, has appointed the Revd. A T Houghton of Mohnyin Upper Burma to be Assistant Bishop of the Diocese…Mr Houghton hopes to leave for Rangoon in June', which reflected the situation as known. It was the beginning of a period of danger and anxiety, punctuated by air raids on Bristol and its surroundings, many changes of plan by the ecclesiastical authorities and far-reaching events in Burma brought about by the Japanese invasion in 1942. S F Russell, a participant in the sufferings of the diocese after 1942, who wrote of his own escape in *Muddy Exodus*, described the effects: 'the tide of war affected northern Burma and Arakan more than the rest of the diocese...the Rising Sun of Japan cast a baleful shadow across the East. By sea and air or on foot across the ranges missionaries escaped from Burma. Houses and churches were destroyed, hospitals deserted or burnt. It was a tragic tale, but the Church of Christ suffered, endured and emerged into a new age. Its foundation was the unshakeable Rock that is Christ' (*Full Fifty Years*, pp.18-19). For Tim and Coralie it was a sad and troubling turn of events, which left them in a spiritual and personal limbo, perhaps as searching as any part of their pilgrimage.

Maggie, the BCMS elephant, who played an important part in evacuating missionaries in 1942

The Houghton Family
taken in Ealing in 1946
(back row left to right) Betty, Pat, Monica
(front row) Beryl, Tim, Michael, Coralie, Rachel

CHAPTER 6

WAR, SHIPWRECK AND FRESH DIRECTIONS 1940-1945

The year of 1940 was one of national crisis. There was the possibility of imminent invasion, the heroism of the Battle of Britain in the skies, Winston Churchill's defiant broadcasts to the nation round the theme 'we will never surrender' and the suffering by a civilian population in war on an unprecedented scale through the intensive bombing of the cities, with many incendiary attacks resulting in large-scale fires. Civilians, Tim Houghton among them, were drafted into volunteer groups as fire-watchers and observers. He recorded that Bristol, where the family had made their home for the furlough, endured over 200 raids in 1940, at its worst five in a single night. For this text, an important source are the daily diaries that Tim Houghton kept from 1940, the earlier ones having been lost through the Japanese invasion of Burma: bracketed dates in the text refer to the diary entries of the year. It is little wonder that he wrote at the end of 1940: 'so we have come to the end of another year – perhaps the strangest and most uncertain year of my life' (December 31, 1940).

There were various strands to this uncertainty. First and most prominent to him was uncertainty relating to his call as bishop. Bishop West faced difficulties in the diocese and even contemplated resignation, which would have left the appointment in the hands of a successor. Tim commented: 'unless he is *forced* into resignation, thro' (sic) the absolute refusal of people to cooperate, it seems very strange that he should give up, and having got as far as obtaining the Metropolitan's consent it does not seem right that he shd. (sic) go back on my appointment' (February 23). He wrote that he retained 'a deep conviction that God means me to go back to Burma, though when and how I cannot say'. He learned on March 11 from a letter that the bishop, publicly challenged to resign, had consulted with the Metropolitan and decided to stay. Tim Houghton was left in a quandary over the announcement of his own appointment by apparently conflicting signals. A cable from the bishop of March 16 confirmed the bishop's stance and asked Tim Houghton, if still willing to come, to arrange a press announcement in the *Times*. This duly appeared on March 21 under the heading 'Assistant Bishop of Rangoon' in the terms we have seen. On April 8th, Coralie received a telegram in his absence setting the date of April 25 for his consecration. Initially this was to happen in London by arrangement with the Archbishop of Canterbury, Cosmo Lang, and required a hasty visit to the ecclesiastical outfitters, Wippells: but on April 15 'Cosmo Cantuar' had ruled that the Metropolitan should consecrate in India, probably in Calcutta on Tim's journey back to Burma. Even in 1940 there were moments of light relief. Wippells arrived for a fitting of his frock coat and purple cassock, observed by Coralie and Monica, who asked: 'Daddy, have you been trying on your *proud* clothes?' (April 15). Lang himself had felt that Orpen's portrait of him made him look proud, pompous and prelatical, prompting Hensley Henson to ask to which of the descriptions 'your Grace takes exception'. Tim Houghton was all too aware of the dangers: 'St Paul would not have cared two hoots whether people knew about him and his work, as long as he served God faithfully. I long to be…completely free from desire for self advancement' (March 21).

Ecclesiastical uncertainties were by no means over in April; August and October were now canvassed as possible dates of consecration in a cable from Bishop West. Apart from the disappointment of further postponement, Tim Houghton was also faced with financial implications: 'we cannot *afford* to continue much longer on a BCMS furlough salary' (April 25). Between April 1940 and his final departure for Burma in March 1941 there were numerous offers of passages to Burma to address and cancel as the situation fluctuated, with the constant emotional see-saw of anticipation and frustration. Frequent raids on the city threatening their safety as a family added to the pressures: night after night there were air raid warnings, meaning the need to move the children downstairs to comparative safety, while Coralie stayed awake with them until the bombing subsided. It was a form of sleep-deprivation which Tim Houghton himself felt to be self-defeating. A double raid on June 25 confirmed the need to paper over the windows against splintering glass but on August 12th an adjoining house belonging to their friends, the Cousins, was hit and shattered by the first 'whistling bomb' to land on Bristol. It fell at the end of their gardens and blew a huge boulder over the Cousins' house into the Houghton's front garden, shattering their windows. He wrote: 'a crash almost on top of us' which left enough debris outside 'to have killed 100 people, but no one had even a scratch!' He got to bed at 3am and was greatly impressed by the immediacy of the re-building, which started at 8am: in addition to which, their housing had visits from Civil Defence, the Home Office and the Minister of Health to investigate: 'by the evening the glass in our downstairs rooms had been put in' and the Cousins' roof 'temporarily covered' (August 12). Various people filed past to see the site of one of the early bombs on Bristol, which also resulted in a special collection being made for the Red Cross.

It was hardly surprising that, under these conditions, the relationship between husband and wife, though continuing strong and loving, came under increasing strain. Coralie found the incessant bombing very hard to bear. For the family's safety she wanted to withdraw to the comparative peace of Limpley Stoke, where her aunts Ella and May were always ready to receive the family. Tim's reaction was to resist this suggestion: as a patriot, he felt that they should not retreat from danger (his doctor sister, Biddy, was indeed in the thick of it in war-torn Bristol): and as a father he wanted the family in its own home with, importantly, access to the younger children's day schools, Pat being a boarder at Monkton Combe. Tension extended further to dispute over his future: to Coralie, now faced with a family of five children and war-time perils, his place was with them and she was deeply reluctant to concede his calling back to Burma as a bishop. Tim grappled with what was, or was not, the will of God in such circumstances; he showed an exemplary attitude in his willingness to subordinate himself to his wife's anxieties but knew that his heart was in Burma and that he had been called to serve the church there. It was a classic, if highly extreme, example of the double vocation to ordained ministry and marriage and family life, played out in conditions of exceptional intensity and debilitating uncertainty. A lesser man might well have been reduced to a breakdown.

It may have been something of a relief to engage himself in extensive deputation work from Bristol for BCMS, often with the family lodged at Limpley Stoke. Those who can remember the conditions of war-time travel, packed and often cold trains with frequently greatly lengthened journeys will be amazed at his stamina as a travelling speaker. Between February and December 1940 he covered most of the country visiting churches and other meetings of BCMS, often staying nights in vicarages to do so: in the north, this meant visits to Liverpool, Blackburn, Ormskirk, Sheffield, Nottingham and Manchester, Leyland and Oldham: in the Midlands, Coventry, Burton-on-Trent and Birmingham; in the south, coastal places like Bexhill, Weymouth, Plymouth to name a selection. He made some sixty visits, which could include 2-3 nights in a setting and he managed to intersperse them with visits to his father at Whitington in Norfolk, who was ageing but still a source of inspiration to him. He certainly earned his furlough stipend from BCMS. Additional visits to Oxford for the OICCU, staying at Oriel College in May, and an IVF missionary conference at Birmingham also in the spring, were unrecognised pointers to the future.

Heavy raids on Bristol blew out the windows of the BCMS college and the main offices at 14, Victoria Street in London received a direct hit (September 19). In November Bristol had its worst raid to date when 'the whole city seemed to be on fire' (November 24), a raid that destroyed most of the city centre including the stores of Boots and Marks and Spencer. After further uncertainties over Burma a passage that was acceptable to them both was agreed by Tim, giving him time to dismantle their Bristol home and store their possessions at Limpley Stoke. Since July he had been in receipt of a bishop's stipend, so the immediate financial need was relieved, and the family were settled in schools, Pat excelling at hockey, rugby and cricket at Monkton Combe, with Betty and Rachel at Bristol High School for Girls. Arrangements were in place for Coralie, Monica, Beryl and Michael to join him in Burma as opportunity permitted, though at this stage he was told no family passages were permitted. The good offices of the CBMS (Conference of British Missionary Societies) with its headquarters at Edinburgh House in London, secured his own passage (March 10, 1941). Raids on the Liverpool docks were to delay his ship but he made his final farewells to the family on March 23, on the eve of the third National Day of Prayer, launched by George VI in a broadcast of May 24, 1940 and strongly approved by Tim. Now he was faced with a lengthy separation, with Coralie, Betty and Rachel all in tears: 'how heartrending it all is! ... Monica came down because she cannot sleep. She has brought me some chocolate and wants me to kiss my hand every night when I go to bed and think of her – she will kiss my photo' (March 23).

On board the MV Staffordshire he was pleased to find that he was sharing a cabin with another BCMS volunteer called Meadows, bound for Burma. A Dr. Howard Jeffry, a medical missionary, was also on board with many Indian and Chinese passengers. Tim noticed the Bofors anti-aircraft gun and Bren guns on the deck but there was plainly no convoy or destroyer escort. The captain revealed that they were bound for Freetown in Sierra Leone. Somewhere south of Iceland in the Atlantic on the first morning out at 11am they were picked up by a German plane and bombed. The first bomb made a 'terrific crash' he wrote in his typed account 'The Shipwrecked Mariner' (p. 9). He wrote that one of his 'greatest underlying dreads' throughout his life had been shipwreck. Faced with the imminent possibility of drowning however 'a wonderful peace immediately seemed to pour into my soul' a peace from God to whom he committed himself. The first bomb had killed a number including two children from one family and a second blew the captain from one side of the bridge to the other without serious effect. After a difficult descent by the rope ladder towards a life-boat, he was encouraged to climb up again as the boat had moved, physically a very demanding challenge which got him into a boat with the most severely injured, to whom he ministered with prayer and encouragement, especially one, a Mrs Ballard, whose hip had been shattered. Great waves meant all were in danger of being washed overboard and in that respect he was glad that his legs were immovable owing to the bodies spread over them. As he began to wonder how any could survive the night under these conditions, someone glimpsed masts on the horizon. A Norwegian ship had picked up their distress signals sent to Wick by the radio operator before the radio mast had been destroyed: 'I began to pray silently that God would incline the heart of the captain ....to make first for our lifeboat' so that the badly injured would get treatment 'some of whom would not survive unless their injuries could be treated soon. God wonderfully answered this prayer' (pp. 17-18). They were rescued at 4.30pm and later that day he had a service of thanksgiving (p. 21). In total some 250 had been rescued, a figure which included crew and naval ratings.

They put in at Stornaway, Isle of Lewis on March 29, 1941 where special arrangements were made for survivors to sleep in the Town Hall. On Sunday he was able to use this building for a service and preached on Psalm 40:2-3 'he brought me up out of the horrible pit', using his earlier experience of being saved from drowning in 1911 as an illustration and pressing home the message that their rescue was for a purpose in their individual lives (p. 29). A Police Sergeant present 'wrung my hand and said that he would not have missed the service for anything'. He proceeded via the Kyle of Lochalsh where all received warrants for travel as 'Shipwrecked Mariners' to a train at Inverness but a telegram to Coralie vastly underestimated the stated time of arrival: snowdrifts meant that the train was already seven hours late at Carlisle. The next day, nine days after the tearful farewells, he was reunited with the family and was greeted too by a cable from Bishop West, telling him now to stay in England for the duration of the war, followed by a letter congratulating him on his courage and resourcefulness over the shipwreck: 'I hear of your magnificent courage on the ship', a well-deserved meed of praise.

For the sake of clarity, the long running saga of the bishopric can be concluded here. Following his advice to Tim to stay in England, Bishop West was himself involved in a serious car accident in Rangoon in June 1941, spent some time in the USA and on his return to Burma reached a decision that, under the exigencies of the war and its effects on the diocese, outlay of another bishop was not affordable. He communicated this to Tim in a letter of October 12, 1943. The bishop's hope was that he would continue to serve in Burma as leader of the BCMS mission, who would pay for him, but by then Wilfred (Bill) Crittle had taken on leadership. Tim Houghton wrote a full and dignified response to this change of policy in a letter of February 29, 1944, where he expressed his sense of a broken and solemn undertaking and its personal effects on himself, above all in denying him a return to Burma: 'I know you want me to speak frankly – I do feel that wrong has been done and the way you have represented your decision, for it seems to me to be a one-sided breaking of a solemn agreement, which not only prevented me from taking up the appointment for which I had been consciously preparing for the last four years but in the particular circumstances in which I find myself bars me entirely from returning to Burma. This is the hardest burden to bear. My decision to respond to your clear call (which seemed to me to be of God) in May 1939 is seen now to have resulted in severing me from work in Burma altogether and if I could have foreseen that at the time it is quite certain I should never have given up the work I was doing'. To Tim the bishop had acted *ultra vires,* needing the agreement of the Metropolitan (obtained), the Diocesan Council and the General Council of the diocese by its constitution under chapter 7 and Canon XI, some of whom had not been consulted. Without intention to do so, the bishop 'had wronged a fellow Christian' by an arbitrary decision.

In reply the bishop defended the decision as shared by the Metropolitan and by 'responsible members of the diocese': he felt that 'the more swiftly and decisively I acted, the kinder I was being to you'. He added: 'for me, what is going to be the crowning triumph is the splendid way in which you are taking it' (May 2, 1944). Less happy, here and earlier, were suggestions of thwarted ambition on Tim's part, which detached judges may feel that the bishop was in no position to make to a fellow Christian so excessively tried by circumstances, while seeking hard to discern the will of God in profoundly troubling times. The whole affair of the bishopric from 1939-44 was an extended trial, requiring monumental forbearance on Tim Houghton's part as bishop designate, as missionary in waiting and as husband and father, where the grace of God prevailed.

As we have seen, during 1940 Tim Houghton had been drawn into the growing work of the IVF. He had participated in the missionary conference in Birmingham held at Selly Oak in April (5-7) and he had been impressed by the high level of input. Faced as he was with finding some employment for the duration of the war after his shipwreck, he was very interested by the suggestion of Dr. Douglas Johnson of the IVF that he might give 50% of his time to them while continuing with deputation for BCMS. The IVF proposal of May 16, 1941 was 'about working in universities to arouse missionary interest'. Dr. Johnson had offered £250 (May 22, 1941), hoping that this could be matched by BCMS, which it was (May 29), with the BCMS committee regarding the approach as a call from God. This was the background to his work in the universities from 1941-1945, some of it later from a base in Cambridge as a staff member of the Round Church (Holy Sepulchre), a centre of evangelical witness in the university.

This is not the place for extensive treatment of the IVF/SCM division, set out by Douglas Johnson himself in his *Contending for the Faith: a history of the Evangelical Movement in the Universities and Colleges* (IVP, 1979) which built on the previous work edited by F.D. Coggan, later Archbishop of Canterbury, *Christ and the Colleges* (1934). Suffice it to say that on a number of important occasions the leadership of the evangelical bodies failed to be reassured that certain Christian essentials were still held as central by the SCM, a conviction that led to division which dated back to 1910 (Johnson, pp. 69ff). A recent and generous assessment of this debate by Robin Boyd, *The Witness of the Student Christian Movement: Church Ahead of the Church* (SPCK, 2007), while drawing attention to missionary giants like Lesslie Newbigin who owed their faith and missionary commitment to the SCM, gives additional credibility to those who judged SCM to be insufficiently rooted in the bible: commenting on the position in the 1970's, Boyd, who himself owed much to SCM, wrote: 'the near collapse of the SCM in the 1970's was largely due, not to bad exegesis but to the rejection of exegesis….the SCM has still some way to go before it can recover its former confident access to the world of biblical and theological academic scholarship' (p. 184). Historical hindsight can justify the anxieties of evangelicals that Biblical doctrine and devotion ran the risk of being swamped by wider social, political and philosophical concerns. Even in 1941 Tim Houghton was to get a taste of these underlying tensions, when the veteran missionary Mildred Cable had suggested a collaboration with the SCM, so causing 'a lot of upset', at a time when he 'heard of the SCM difficulties, and also the CMS jealousy about the IVF who really seem to think they ought to have the monopoly of men at Oxford and Cambridge' (June 7, 1941).

Tim Houghton himself continued to put the emphasis on stirring up missionary interest in the universities as a travelling secretary when confronted by attempts to direct him into student evangelism (June 19). He remained very impressed by the high intellectual calibre of those involved. At a gathering in July 1941 those present included G T Manley, sometime fellow of Christ's College, Cambridge, Professor Maclean, Principal of New College, Edinburgh, Dr Martyn Lloyd-Jones, Professor Martin who held the chair of Semitic Languages at Liverpool and F F Bruce, then teaching as professor of Greek at Leeds. Tim wrote of his enthusiasm for the signs of 'a renewal of Biblical Theology', which he found 'really refreshing'. There was criticism of the kind of evangelicalism which Lloyd-Jones in particular typified as 'Moodyism and Keswick' in character, which had resulted in an 'anti-intellectualism and lack of systematic theology'

(July 8). It was an atmosphere where his own inherited Calvinism was at ease. By July 19th Douglas Johnson had given him a skeleton programme for visits to university groups and a large sheaf of papers to study relating to the IVF. He was also commissioned to write a pamphlet to replace R P Wilder's *Bible and Foreign Missions*, which he regarded as a 'very slipshod affair' (June 19). His own pamphlet was entitled 'The Battle for World Evangelisation', which encountered some criticism for its excessive use of the military metaphor from G T Manley, but was ultimately produced by the IVF (July 3, 10-15; August 14, 16 1941).

One opening which was to give him much satisfaction over twenty-five years was an invitation to conduct confirmation classes for the 300 girls of Clarendon School, then near Malvern. Miss Swain, the headmistress, who belonged herself to the Plymouth Brethren, had great confidence in Tim Houghton as a Christian teacher: and although this led to some tension with W W Cash, once CMS general secretary and then Bishop of Worcester and the confirming bishop, who may have resented a BCMS incursion and preferred the local incumbent, eventually he accepted the headmistress' wish with some grace (August 30, 1944). Betty and Rachel became boarders at the school and so their parents were able to combine visits for classes with overnight stays to see their daughters. Tim took his duties with great seriousness, often at some inconvenience but it was plainly a fulfilling element in his ministry.

As with his deputation work for BCMS, the IVF work involved extensive travel. His brief included the Scottish, Welsh and Irish universities, responsibilities shared with another travelling secretary in Miss Bennett, along with many English institutions. This could mean more long train journeys to Edinburgh and Aberdeen, not to mention ferry crossings to Dublin and Belfast, where he faced the additional hazards of searching enquiry from custom officials. Dublin in war-time amazed him with bright street lights after blackouts and goods in shops quite unobtainable in England (March 4, 1942). He set himself high standards in terms of numbers of speaking engagements on these visits, addressing many different groups: with two Sunday sermons added to other occasions he could speak on five occasions on one day. Contemporary readers will be surprised at the numbers of his hearers: while he could be disappointed by a congregation of one hundred in a church in Oxford, he often spoke to meetings of some hundreds elsewhere and in the case of YMCA gatherings in Ireland to thousands, although many meetings for student groups were of ten or twenty. One visit which he plainly delighted in making was to his old student haunts in Durham. Here he preached at St Nicholas for W.S.F. Pickering, addressed a Christian Union meeting (DICCU) on the calling to overseas service, was entertained at the deanery by Dean Alington where he spoke to a meeting of 150 on his experience of shipwreck (and was assured by the dean of the prayers of the cathedral) and preached later for Canon Wallis, principal of St John's and rector of St Mary-le-Bow (November 21-23, 1941). He reflected: 'certainly I have seen no college yet (not even Oxford and Cambridge) which in any ways compares in my estimation to this glorious pile of buildings' (November 21). His Sunday finished with an informal discussion at St Mary's College on comparative religion and the problems of opium addiction. It was hardly surprising that, after a similar set of meetings at Belfast, in 1942, he wrote: 'felt very tired tonight' after meetings which had included addressing two thousand people for the YMCA: it was both 'very encouraging' (March1) but also exhausting: 'felt very tired this morning – perhaps I really need a rest!' (March 11), no doubt not helped by news of the Japanese invasion of Rangoon, which he recorded on March 10, 1942.

The list of universities for his first itinerary was indeed daunting enough. In addition to those noticed he was to cover London, Liverpool, Manchester, Reading, Sheffield, Birmingham, Bristol, Cambridge, Nottingham, Oxford, Leeds, Newcastle, Hull, Lancaster and Loughborough during the first term of the academic year 1941/2. He was subject to the vagaries of student arrangements of which he had been warned by Dr. Johnson. These could involve last minute change of plan, when a meeting understood to be a small Christian group instead became a widely advertised university meeting on Burma, chaired by the principal. After working as a travelling secretary, he accepted the title suggested by Douglas Johnson of missionary secretary (March 25, 1943). By November 1943, in the absence of any openings in Burma, he agreed to consider becoming assistant secretary of the IVF to Dr Johnson and this was finally agreed in 1944 with a financial package of £750 (January 28, 1944). A house belonging to the veteran evangelical, Basil Atkinson, under-librarian of the university library in Cambridge, had been promised for the family (November 12, 1943) but this arrangement fell through. Eventually, after a long period at Limpley Stoke, a house in Madingley Road, Cambridge became their family home and they moved in during June 1944. The Bishop of Ely invited him to take responsibility for the Round Church and he began his ministry there in December and wrote 'I had a very happy six months there' with a small parish and student support from Oliver Barclay who by then had failed his attempt to become a Fellow of Trinity but was embarked on a doctoral course (October 8, 20, 1944) and became a lay reader at the Round Church (December 13, 1944; April 30, 1945).

Although wholly in sympathy with the IVF and its Basis of Faith and ways of working, there were occasions when he demurred at the opinions expressed. It was too much for Tim Houghton to refer to the SCM, as Oliver Barclay did at an IVF meeting, as 'the enemy camp': 'not quite fair to a body of those who at least profess to be Christians', though he remained in sympathy with the policy of non-cooperation with 'those who are not concerned with the Truth as we know it' (September 19, 1942). By the same token he baulked at an address by the IVF speaker, Dr Martyn Cundy, who 'was a little too slashing about Rome' (April 8, 1943), when some RC students were present at the conference involved. He was prepared to disagree with the doyen of IVF speakers, Martyn Lloyd-Jones, whose deliverances he greatly admired, on the subject of patriotism: unlike Lloyd-Jones, he did not see 'mystic loyalty to the Crown' as a 'form of idolatry', practised among the English but not by Celts: 'I crossed swords with him and we have had a very interesting discussion which went on till nearly 12.30am'.

Attempts were made in 1943 and 1944 to draw him towards other work. Canon Mohan of the CPAS had approached him in December 1942 to join the staff. Now Bishop Stuart of Uganda, who had both benefited from the East African Revival and also suffered from some divisive tendencies, in company with the lay missionary Algy Stanley-Smith, pressed him to become assistant bishop, as someone who would have the confidence of the revivalists and also act as a corrective leader when needed. He found this offer attractive (November 15, 1944), combining missionary service with church leadership. While he was still considering it, however, he was alerted by BCMS supporters that, were Dr Bartlett to retire, he would be very welcome as the new general secretary of BCMS. After a lengthy period of meetings, consultations, and much internal debate, not least caused by Dr Bartlett's changes of mind and basic unwillingness to relinquish the reins of office, he was finally installed as general secretary. He had taken his dilemma to the Archbishop of Canterbury (March 3, 1945). Earlier

William Temple had shown great sympathy with his position over the Burma bishopric and now Geoffrey Fisher, after Temple's tragically early death, who plainly saw the strategic importance of the Ruanda offer from Bishop Stuart, with some reluctance accepted that only Tim Houghton himself could weigh up the conflicting demands of central Africa and the BCMS appointment (May 15, 1945). The offer of the Ruanda work was made in January 1945 but refused (February 8th) among other things providing a final refutation that simple episcopal preferment was ever his aim. At a meeting chaired by Basil Atkinson, who 'surpassed himself with masterly and good humoured chairmanship' held on July 10, 1945, Dr Bartlett's agreement to resign was finally accepted and his successor's appointment put in hand. His position as assistant secretary of the IVF was filled in due course by Oliver Barclay, by then holder of a Ph.D. He himself embarked on twenty-one years of service to BCMS, after serving an equivalent period as a BCMS missionary in the field.

CHAPTER 7

BCMS GENERAL SECRETARY: MISSIONARY STRATEGY AND DIRECTION 1945 - 1966

Before launching into the next 21 years of service to BCMS, two vignettes from Tim Houghton's daily diaries may serve to set the scene for his stance in those years. In the first, he was in conversation with Geoffrey Fisher, Archbishop of Canterbury at Lambeth Palace, about the possibility of the Ruanda episcopate, pressed on him by Bishop Stuart and Algy Stanley-Smith. He took the opportunity to lay out his stall as an evangelical churchman: 'at one point I told him (Fisher) that while I was intensely Anglican by conviction, I was a "definite Evangelical"'. He said: 'I take off my hat to them…he definitely offered me the job as Ass.Bp. (sic)' (3 March 1945). The second is a conversation with a CMS missionary, Miss Joynt, who had served in China, held at Keswick. This lady told him that she believed he had been preserved in his shipwreck so that CMS and BCMS could unite: 'she said she had thanked God I was torpedoed for now there was a hope of BCMS amalgamating with CMS! I assured her there was nothing of the sort, but I hoped we could continue our work without antagonism' (13 July 1946). The two encounters well illustrate the path he adopted as general secretary of BCMS as a loyal Anglican, a committed evangelical and steward of the distinctiveness of the society he served.

Because he became so central to conservative evangelicalism in those years, characterised at the time of his funeral by John Stott as years of 'evangelical renaissance', it would be all too easy in what follows to forget that his chief preoccupation on a daily basis was administering the life and work of a missionary society whose missionary membership, including spouses and retired missionaries, numbered some 400 people by the early 1970's, as listed by S F Russell in *Full Fifty Years* (pp. 79-89). During Tim Houghton's tenure, the income of the society ranged from £61,000 in 1956 to £100,000 in 1960. He himself was employed on £700 with £100 for allowances for his children (24 July 1945), raised to £950 in 1962, when he commented wryly that his stipend now equalled what he had earned as a staff officer in 1918. The society had work in North Africa, where responsibility for the bishopric caused him much anxiety, not least when Bishop Morris, its occupant, moved to South Africa; in India, Burma, China until evacuation, Iran, Ethiopia and East Africa (Kenya, Uganda, Tanzania), the Arctic and Canada. He was assisted at BCMS headquarters by other secretaries who became his friends as well as colleagues, notably Harold Hacking, who had served with him in Burma, and, when Hacking left for a parochial appointment in September 1953, by J E Seddon, hymn writer, musician and BCMS secretary in North Africa from 1945: he was appointed as Home Secretary on October 26, 1954. Eustace Davies served as Overseas Secretary after service in West China (1936-52). Two strongly supportive figures on BCMS committees were W L (Bill) Leathem, who became vicar of St John's, Harborne in this period, and whom Tim regarded as a firm friend with whom he could disagree but retain deep bonds of friendship; and Osmond Peskett, missionary in China (1934-51), vicar of St Stephen's, Tonbridge and later missionary in Tanzania (1965-7), both wise and valued advisors. After being bombed out of 14, Victoria Street, BCMS moved to no. 96 before having offices in Romney Street and Clapham, culminating after Tim's time in the building in the Waterloo Road built by CMS, an arrangement for a shared base negotiated with other societies like SAMS by Tim Houghton himself. His own house was in Ealing (9, Ascott Avenue) from 1945-60, where he attended the church of St John's, West Ealing and Coralie served on the PCC, often meeting with Professor Norman Anderson on Sundays, before moving to a house near Christ Church, Cockfosters (46, Bramley Rd.) when he found himself often worshipping with members of the Oakhill college staff during the principalship of M A P (Maurice) Wood.

A flavour of a typical day at work was given by the diary entry of 12 September 1951: 'feeling very tired this morning, but had to get up just the same....I got out the agenda for the East Africa Field sub com. (sic) next week, and then dictated letters to the Turners and Daulbys in the Arctic. Gen. Lucas came along at 11.20...his son...was arranging to send a film strip projector (to the field)...Then Eustace Davis arrived, and we went out to lunch and then talked till nearly 3.0 about China, the CIM and his own future etc. Hazel Thomas...who is training at a London Hospital, came for an interview and I had to write a report afterwards. I looked up some of the Richmond correspondence with a view to drafting a letter. I returned with Harold (Hacking) and got home soon after 6.0...' This provided the background to much wide involvement and further administrative work and leadership in Keswick, the Evangelical Alliance, the embryonic Church of England Evangelical Council and the wider body of the Evangelical Fellowship in the Anglican Communion (EFAC), the BCMS colleges in Bristol, Dalton House for women and what became Tyndale Hall, the Missionary School of Medicine led by Sir John Weir of which Tim was president (1948-77), Weir being a consultant to the royal family, Mount Hermon Missionary Training College (president 1960-71) much involvement with the Alliance Club led by Freddie Crittenden providing for many Asian and African students of differing religions and cultures and, very significantly, the Conference of British Missionary Societies (CBMS), which resulted later in his attendance at the New Delhi WCC meeting of 1961, when the integration of the International Missionary Council and WCC took place. He served also on the Church of England's missionary bodies which answered to the Church Assembly and on an Asia sub-committee, where he met with old Burma hands like Bishop Tubbs and later Bishop George West. He continued his classes for girl confirmands at Clarendon, which meant rail journeys from London to North Wales regularly. He made time to write and in 1956 published *Preparing to be a Missionary* (IVF), an admirable handbook of its kind, which showed him to be abreast of the missionary classics of Roland Allen and Donald McGavran, while also containing much sound scriptural and practical advice based on his own experience. The first edition sold out quickly and he added to it *What of New Delhi?* and *Gospel for the World*, both in 1962.

The missionary statesman J H (Joe) Oldham used to say that 'parties are good for the church', by which he meant that groups of committed people who shared fundamental premises were capable of considerable achievement. This was abundantly true of various small groups of leaders amongst whom he moved. Keswick will largely be handled later but here he worked with such a group after joining the Keswick Council in April 1945. It included Fred Mitchell, Home Secretary of the CIM, Clarence Foster, Hugh Orr-Ewing, 'Sandy' Bradley, W H Aldis, W W Martin and G D (George) Duncan, a blend of laymen and the ordained. General Wilson Haffenden and Major W F (Bill) Batt were also significant figures. Tim became a Keswick trustee in 1947 (16 September 1947) and chairman of the Keswick Council after Fred Mitchell's tragic death in the air crash in 1951. It was a role he fulfilled for 17 years which required considerable administrative expertise when handling some 6,000 people the week of the convention in July.

A further significant group was the so-called IVF 'Church of England' group. Here he met with Hugh Gough, then Bishop of Barking and later Archbishop of Sydney, L F E Wilkinson, principal of Oakhill until his sudden death in harness, Gordon Savage of the Church Society, later Bishop of Buckingham and of Southwell, Alan Stibbs of the Oakhill staff, Maurice Wood, then vicar of St Mary's, Islington, later Bishop of Norwich and Talbot Mohan, the general secretary of the CPAS (Church Pastoral Aid Society). John Stott and Oliver Barclay were also members, as were T.L. Livermore, rector of Morden and Cecil Bewes, Africa Secretary of CMS and later vicar of Tonbridge, like Tim Houghton a Keswick trustee from 1961 and member of the Keswick Council. The group became ultimately the Church of England Evangelical Council but at this early stage was meeting informally in Oliver Barclay's office in Bedford Square (4 July 1946). Tim became chairman in 1960 with R C (Dick) Lucas of St Helen's Bishopsgate as his secretary.

At a discussion in 1959, John Stott raised the subject of the then defunct body, the Central Evangelical Council, of which T L Livermore had the minute book (23 October 1959). In November 1959, Hugh Gough prepared for the launch of an Evangelical Fellowship in the Anglican Communion, of which CEEC would be a member. The Islington Clerical Conference of 12 January 1960 was suggested for this. This conference had always proved a meeting ground for wider evangelicalism, patronised equally by those whom Max Warren had described as 'unhyphenated evangelicals' (neither conservative nor liberal in disposition) as well as the more conservative like Tim Houghton himself. He and Max Warren had a mutually deep and genuine respect for one another, going back many years and during their time as general secretaries of CMS and BCMS. This was evidenced by a letter of appreciation to Tim Houghton at the time of Max's retirement from CMS and was a friendship which meant much to both parties (16 January 1963). Max's attitude to conservative evangelicals was set out by his biographer, F W Dillistone: 'the truth is, of course, that I have their evangelistic commitment and they know that I do', though Dillistone noted that nothing caused Max more perplexity than this relationship (*Into All the World*, pp.154-5). Tim was aware that Max, his brother-in-law Bryan Green, Donald Coggan as principal of the London College of Divinity (later Bishop of Bradford and Archbishop of York) and Sir Kenneth Grubb (with all of whom he shared a meal and fellowship in 1947 (16 October 1947)) were all evangelicals who at this stage did not, in Dillistone's words, share his views of 'the nature and authority of the Bible in any exclusive way' (p.154). Nevertheless, by the end of Tim Houghton's time at BCMS, Max was advising him that BCMS needed to retain its independent identity: 'Max stated categorically that he felt there was a need for the special witness of BCMS, wh. (sic) cd. only be made in independence'. Tim added: 'we discussed many matters of mutual concern – Evangelical continuity etc. & I thoroughly enjoyed the talk' (11 June 1959). When he retired from CMS, Max wrote a 'delightful' letter on Tim Houghton's work and presence at BCMS (29 January 1963).

The early history of CEEC provided an example of whether the broader evangelical constituency was capable of inclusion by the new body. Various bishops had been approached to act as vice-presidents and to Tim's chagrin had declined. Bishop J.R. Taylor, however, who had been principal of Wycliffe Hall and later Bishop of Sodor and Man, was willing to act as president. At a meeting in May 1961, one of the broader group of evangelicals and a speaker at Islington Conferences was proposed for CEEC membership: J P (Jim) Hickinbotham had been vice-principal of Wycliffe Hall and by then, after a spell as professor of theology in Ghana (Gold Coast), was principal of St John's College, Durham. Membership required a high number of votes, which Hickinbotham failed to obtain but this deeply offended Bishop Taylor, who made it clear that if someone of Hickinbotham's type was not welcome he would have to withdraw himself (23 May 1961). John Stott was plainly aware of Bishop Taylor's importance to the new body and urged his retention (12 July 1961). Events were overtaken by his death aged 78 in December of the same year, after which a memorial service was held at All Soul's, Langham Place, attended by Max Warren with Donald Coggan as preacher. Tim Houghton became the first official chair of CEEC in October 1961 (12 October 1961) and the *Church Times* recognised the birth of EFAC and CEEC as a member body with front page treatment in the issue of 20 October 1961.

Conservative evangelicals were riding high in the 1950's, as Adrian Hastings noted in his *History of English Christianity 1922-1990*: 'one part of the Church of England was in good heart and that was its evangelical wing' (p. 453), somewhat symbolised for him by the captain of the English cricket team of 1954, David Sheppard, being ordained in 1955 'product of the old Cambridge Evangelical stable' (p. 447). David Sheppard was to be part of another group in which Tim Houghton shared, which re-constituted the Church of England Newspaper after 1955, serving on an editorial board (29 June 1961). In the 1950's, another group of evangelical leaders were responsible for the invitation to the American evangelist, Billy Graham, who addressed a small group chaired by General Sir Arthur Smith (20 March 1952) when Tim Houghton was 'struck by his humility, balance and determination to cut out emotionalism, sensationalism and anything else which would detract from the preaching of the Word of God'. This group included Hugh Gough and T L Livermore as Anglicans and also leaders from wider evangelicalism like Tom Rees, Martyn Lloyd-Jones, Alan Redpath, George Duncan and John Laird. Graham had been criticised for only reaching the already committed but his organisation was able to reply that 45% of respondents had no previous church affiliation (20 October 1953). This meeting was a prelude to remarkable happenings at the Haringay arena in February-April 1954. Tim recorded attendance of 40,000 on February 27 and a similar figure on March 21. The climax of the campaign came in May, when according to Adrian Hastings (p. 455) attendance at the Wembley stadium was 120,000 with an overspill at the White City of 65,000. Tim and Coralie attended frequently and rejoiced at the thousands who 'came forward' in commitment or enquiry. The *Church Times* might in Tim Houghton's eyes be 'supercilious' in treating Graham's proclamation as only half the gospel; but he and other evangelicals were overjoyed with the preaching and its response. In 1955, seven nights in May produced attendances of 50-60,000 per night at the Wembley stadium, with a final night figure of 80,000. (John Pollock, *Billy Graham*, p.203). Graham addressed a meeting for ministers on May

13 attended by 2000 and went on to conduct a successful mission to the University of Cambridge, when, Norman Anderson reported to Tim, some 500 undergraduates had made professions of faith (20 November 1955). Before that he had been invited by the Queen and the Duke of Edinburgh to lunch at Windsor and to preach there on May 22nd and had been entertained by the Queen Mother and Princess Margaret, when Canon Livermore told Tim Houghton that the Princess had noted changes amongst her friends (22 June 1955). His own account of his meeting with the greatest living Englishman, Winston Churchill, was recorded graphically in his own book *Just as I am*, when he tried to convey to the great statesman, who had described himself as a 'man without hope', for the world and for his own soul, the firm basis in the New Testament for both, after which he was encouraged to pray with him by Churchill (pp.235-7).

The late 1940's and 1950's were a time when the young Houghton family began to mature and marry. Tim and Coralie went through the deep anxieties of many Christian parents. Between 1945-7, to their eyes it seemed that Pat, their eldest son, was in danger of rejecting their profoundly held Christian values and convictions. The daily journal records their deep concern (10 September 1947). All the greater was their joy when, in an entry of 9 June 1948, they 'wept for joy' at what they saw as Pat's return from the far country, which was followed by his attendance at Keswick (19 July 1949) and his engagement to Dorothy Ryan in 1950. Rachel was already engaged to Peter Thompson in 1948 and it must have been very satisfying to Tim and Coralie that in 1954, now married, they followed them to serve in Burma (10 November 1954), where Peter brought his medical skills to the field between 1954-66. With these joys came sorrows: Stan, his brother died very suddenly in China on 17 July 1950 when serving with CIM (10 August 1950), Frank and Dorrie, also with CIM, faced problems with the mission in Shanghai (28 February 1951) which caused their return home; and their father, who had continued to serve in his parish in Norfolk to the age of 90, after retiring to Bath, died in January 1951. Tim had written of him on his 88th birthday: 'we do thank God for his rugged consistency' (2 January 1947). Betty married Peter Simmons, another medical man, in September 1956 and Beryl married Peter Pytches, a Tyndale Hall trained clergyman, in 1958. This left the remaining two, of whom Monica married Campbell Matthews, then working in teaching but subsequently ordained and Michael, who married

Frances in the same year of 1961 after gaining academic awards at both St Paul's and Queen's, Cambridge. What is especially remarkable in this list is that all the children and their spouses shared Tim and Coralie's Christian convictions (rare among such families, if not unknown), which enhanced their joy. There was no more devoted grandparent than Tim Houghton to judge from his diaries. In their turn, the families helped and supported practically and financially in later life, when their parent's sacrificial service meant straitened means for retirement housing and life.

Among his responsibilities was service on the councils of what became Tyndale Hall (before that the BCMS College) and Dalton House. He was always glad to visit his doctoring sister Biddy on trips to Bristol: journeys from London to Bristol were frequent. He had known Dodgson Sykes, principal of the men's college, from his days at the London College of Divinity. Now he found him to be a man under strain (28 January 1947), who dreaded the inspection of the college and was considering resignation. Tim Houghton expressed deep sympathy for Sykes' difficulties (10 July 1947), which seem to have been compounded by a reluctance to have meetings with his staff. Tim felt that he needed much support and encouragement in a difficult role when a crisis developed in October 1950, when Geoffrey Bromiley, future professor at Fuller, translator of Karl Barth's *Dogmatics* and biographer of Dr. Bartlett, was a member of staff (13, 27 October 1950; *Autobiography* p. 861). Eventually Sykes did retire. Talbot Mohan of the CPAS and Alan Stibbs of Oakhill were considered as possible principals and Mohan's refusal is recorded (6 February 1951). Finally, Stafford Wright, whom Tim so nearly recruited for Burma in the 1940's, became principal in 1951. The appointment of J I (Jim) Packer to the staff of Tyndale Hall marked out the college as an attractive training setting for theologically minded evangelicals and his book *Fundamentalism and the Word of God* of 1958 was an important contribution recognised as such by a critic of fundamentalism like Michael Ramsey at the Lambeth Conference of 1958 (23 July 1958). Tim Houghton noted a 'rising tide' of evangelical ordinands (25 March 1955). The proximity of Clifton Theological College in Bristol gave rise as early as 1952 to suggestions of staff exchanges from Alec Motyer, a staff member (1 October 1952). This was an idea whose time was yet to come with a tortuous history towards a merger which stretched beyond Tim's retirement and will be handled then. At this stage merger ideas were resisted equally by a council member of Clifton like E G H (Teddy) Saunders then vicar of Christ Church, Finchley

(15 February 1961); and by Malcolm McQueen, lay member of Tyndale Council, who feared for Tyndale losing its distinctive evangelical emphasis (19, 23 September 1963), although the Clifton principal, Tom Anscombe, was willing enough to enter talks (23 January 1961). Clifton, like Tyndale earlier, faced staff upheavals when two staff members in Peter Dawes, later Bishop of Derby, and Alec Motyer resigned in 1965 and CEEC, appealed to for adjudication, backed the then principal, Basil Gough; but Tim regarded the whole episode as 'tragic' (26 March 1965). McGrath's life of Packer has suggested social, as well as theological, elements at play between the two colleges, Clifton being composed of many from independent schools while Tyndale was more mixed in social background. For whatever reasons, any merger had to wait.

For many, the evangelical commitments mentioned would have proved enough but Tim Houghton also entered a wider circle of Christian leaders after BCMS took up membership of the Conference of British Missionary Societies (CBMS) (15 June 1950). Here he met and worked with people like Ronald Orchard, general secretary of CBMS, Lesslie Newbigin, bishop in the CSI (Church of South India) then working for the International Missionary Council; Norman Goodall past assistant secretary of the WCC, George Appleton later archbishop of Perth, Stephen Neill and David Paton, author of *Christian Missions and the Judgement of God* and secretary of the Missionary and Ecumenical Council of the Church Assembly (MECCA), whose confidence Tim Houghton plainly won and who did his best to promote him as a reliable representative of conservative evangelicals in wider circles. Figures like Willem Visser t'Hooft, general secretary of the WCC, attended CBMS meetings (10 February 1958), with others like C.W. Ransom of the Theological Education Fund and Hendrik Kraemer, the Dutch lay theologian and missionary. Tim Houghton was warmly appreciative of Lesslie Newbigin, his leadership, spirituality and theological depth and incisiveness. He himself won the respect of these leaders, not least in the debates over whether or not the IMC was to merge with the WCC, opposed by Max Warren, of which Newbigin was the chief protagonist. Tim Houghton made a statesmanlike speech at the University of St Andrews, prior to the New Delhi meeting of the WCC, where this was to be decided (12 August 1960): 'I spoke as a conservative evangelical, whose society had opposed...I then spoke on the other side – all that had been done to remove misgivings, the definition of the Commission which was theologically satisfying and the proposed elaboration of the WCC

Basis to bring in Scripture and the Holy Trinity. In view of the general acceptance and the strong support of the younger churches, I felt one ought to hope for a climate in which the standpoint I represented wd. (sic) be welcomed and therefore proposed to vote for acceptance'. This speech was warmly welcomed by Bishop Chandu Ray and Tim Houghton was thanked by Visser t'Hooft, Norman Goodall and Bishop Newbigin among others, which he found 'quite embarrassing'. The Swedish missionary bishop and theological professor, Bengt Sundkler, asked for a copy of the speech before leaving for Nairobi the next day, in order to be able to quote it. The result of the vote at St Andrews was unanimous, which explains the enthusiasm of the proponents for his support.

With the backing of, among others, Max Warren, Tim Houghton found himself among the handful of delegates from the CBMS for the New Delhi meeting, itself a mark of respect. In the wider evangelical world at home, however, this provoked criticism, not least from Dr Martyn Lloyd-Jones, who regarded his attendance at such a gathering as compromising to evangelicalism, referring to it as a 'major disaster to the Evangelical cause' (9 February 1962), a position vigorously rebutted by Tim Houghton, who noted that similar considerations had not prevented Lloyd-Jones serving on the British Council of Churches. Tim pointed to his involvement in mixed settings in Burma where no loss of principle or compromise was involved. He heard a violent attack on the WCC by the evangelical H Legerton (1 May 1962) and was aware that some of his close IVF friends like Douglas Johnson, as with Lloyd-Jones, would have nothing to do with the WCC. When Herbert Carson taxed him with J C Ryle's writings, the doughty evangelical Bishop of Liverpool of late Victorian days, he pointed rightly to Ryle's involvement in mixed meetings known as Church Congresses, where he too made his contribution without compromise. Altogether he was firm under criticism and urged his fellow evangelicals to become more involved in ecumenism. The New Delhi meeting (November 15 – December 9, 1961) brought him in touch with church leaders from all over the world and resulted in many invitations to speak both to evangelical and more mixed contexts, while his written account *What of New Delhi?* was begun soon after his return and published in 1962.

Probably the most explosive and divisive development in Tim's final years at BCMS was the sudden appearance of what has become known as the charismatic movement, with the particular phenomenon of speaking in tongues. Tim Houghton was aware that Michael Harper, John Stott's curate at All Soul's, Langham Place had embraced the practice and there are references to it in Dagenham (27 April 1961), Bristol (30 April 1961) and at the BCMS conference at Herne Bay, Kent (1 May 1961). He was troubled by it and wrote of John Stott's former senior curate, John Collins, and his curates David Macinnes and David Watson, who had entered into the experience after a night of prayer, that it was 'sinister'. His use of language is revealing: occurrences at Clarendon were labelled 'an outbreak', as if of some infectious disease. He shared the reaction of John Stott and the IVF with him of a theological wariness of the phenomenon, expressed judiciously in Stott's address to the Islington Conference of 1964, which became a widely read booklet, 'The Baptism and Fullness of the Holy Spirit'. He was told by John Skinner of the IVF staff that some one third of CU's were involved (20 June 1964) but by later that year Skinner judged that the issue had subsided (8 November 1964). His own wariness was only heightened by being told by the widow of a respected Keswick leader of an 'outbreak' in York some time before which had made her 'quite certain' that 'tongues were of the devil' (9 July 1964). One result of his suspicion of charismatics was that while he was chairman of Keswick speakers of the calibre of David Watson, David Macinnes and David Pawson, known charismatics, were deliberately not invited. An address and pamphlet written for the Protestant Reformation Society, entitled 'The Work of the Holy Spirit in the Church Today' (May 1974) continued to show hesitations about the movement ('neo-pentecostal'), which he saw as a cause of disunity and division, a refuge of the mentally unstable, while conceding that it had been the source of blessing for 'many' in 'their own spiritual lives' (p.12; pp. 12-14).

One final issue of some complexity occupied his attention in the 1960's. The Church of England and the Methodist Church had produced a scheme aimed to unite the two bodies. In South India, the successful scheme which produced the Church of South India, had accepted the two different ordained ministries during an interim period, after which all ordinations were to be conducted by bishops: episcopal ordination therefore became the norm but not at once. This had proved a stumbling block to certain Anglicans and, when the Anglican-Methodist scheme was produced, a special service of reconciliation was included, with mutual laying on of hands by both Methodist leaders and Anglican bishops – if high church Anglicans wished to interpret this as ordination in the 'historic succession' of bishops they were free to do so. Evangelical critics were understandably concerned that such a procedure down-graded Methodist orders, was based on a theological 'fudge' open to a deliberately varied set of interpretations and introduced to the process a view of ordination based on a theologically suspect doctrine of 'apostolical succession'. Much hinged on questions of theological proportion: was the gain of organic unity so great that proportionately the varied understandings of the service could be tolerated?

As chairman of CEEC, Tim Houghton was confronted by stern critics of the scheme in Jim Packer, Colin Buchanan and Gervase Duffield, lay member of the Church Assembly. Ultimately this resulted in the combined Anglo-Catholic-Evangelical publication *All in each Place* (1965), in which Packer and Buchanan shared authorship with Graham Leonard, later Bishop of London, and Eric Mascall, able theologian. Opposing views were expressed at CEEC meetings: as chairman Tim Houghton had to admit to 'fundamental disagreement' on it (13 March 1964). When he and Maurice Wood, as members of the council, supported the report, along with such evangelicals as Teddy Saunders, Michael Green and Martin Parsons (26 February 1964), Packer wrote of them in the Church of England Newspaper of 17 July 1964: 'they view their evangelicalism as simply a party view in the Church of England and do not object in principle to the Church's official actions being determined by Anglo-Catholic convictions about the ministry...their reactions...leave one wondering whether 'Broad Church Pietists' would not be a better description of some than 'Evangelicals''. Such an approach did not prevent Packer and Buchanan from combining with Anglo-Catholics in a book which did much to undermine the scheme: but it should be added that Methodists too had their dissentient voices: C.K. Barrett, Professor of New Testament at Durham and T E Jessop, past professor of philosophy at Hull, two of the ablest minds in Methodism, remained unconvinced. To Tim Houghton, however, some of Packer and Buchanan's objections (for example, against any service of reconciliation) would prove fatal to many unity schemes with which he was familiar: 'though we discussed amicably I found there was a fundamental divergence with Packer and Buchanan...not...prepared to back any scheme of reunion which has a unification rite at the beginning: that would cut out Ceylon, North India, Pakistan, Nigeria and Ghana and seems to me completely unrealistic' (20 November 1964). It was a sign of his largeness of mind and his ecumenical and missionary spirit that he was seriously concerned about the effects of such theological rigorism on the younger churches and their unity schemes.

Towards the end of his time at BCMS there were concerted moves to see that his sterling service to the church was recognised, largely initiated by Harry Sutton the general secretary of SAMS, who greatly admired Tim. He confessed that what would have been most welcome would have been the on-going recognition from the church in Burma: but, in the absence of that, he was clearly greatly honoured and pleased to be made an honorary canon of the new cathedral and diocese of Morogoro in Tanzania, where the influence of his old friend and collaborator, the Australian bishop Alfred Stanway, who had drawn BCMS into Tanzania, was the moving spirit. Although it proved impossible for him to attend his installation in the cathedral, it was recognition which was richly deserved and gratefully appreciated (15, 28 June 1965). It was coupled and complemented by his choice as preacher of the CMS Annual Sermon (30 June 1966), almost inconceivable for someone in his position thirty years earlier and a mark of esteem. In September 1966 came the final meetings when he attended his last Standing Committee as general secretary when a presentation was made by cheque and the valedictory meeting at Partridge Hall in Church House, presided by his successor in post, Alan Neech, when further presentations were made at what he described as 'a lovely meeting' of BCMS supporters and family members (27 September 1966). So ended 21 years of dedicated and effective missionary leadership of the society.

CHAPTER 8

KESWICK AND KEELE

Tim Houghton's involvement in the Keswick Convention continued after his retirement from BCMS: he remained chairman from 1951 to 1969. Some background to the convention is needed to indicate what this meant to him and many others. The convention had developed out of the vision of a vicar of Keswick, Canon Harford-Battersby, in 1875. It was largely the result of the visit to England of two American Quakers, Hannah and Robert Pearsall Smith, whose teaching on the spiritual life had impressed Harford-Battersby. He and a layman friend, Robert Wilson, himself a Quaker who also taught in a Baptist Sunday School and who lived near Cockermouth at Broughton Grange, initiated the convention with the assistance of men like Evan Hopkins, vicar of Holy Trinity, Richmond from 1871 and Hanmer Webb-Peploe, who became a long serving vicar of St Paul's, Onslow Square for forty-three years. The aim was to promote 'practical and scriptural holiness'. An important additional influence in the 1880's was Handley Moule, who after initial hesitations became an advocate of Keswick and who became in turn principal of Ridley Hall, Cambridge, a professor in the university and finally Bishop of Durham. For some time, partly through fears that the societies would jockey for position and finance at the convention, missionary societies and their emphasis were not welcome but this was reversed as a policy in the late 1880's, after which Keswick became a formidable force and recruiting ground for the missionary societies, not least, through the adherence of its secretary and historian Eugene Stock, the CMS.

Tim Houghton's immediate predecessors as chairman were W H Aldis, whom he greatly respected and regarded as 'unshakeable', who died in June 1948, and Fred Mitchell, Home Secretary of the CIM, who was killed tragically in an air crash in 1951. It was with some considerable shrinking of spirit and sense of inadequacy that he discovered that the other Keswick leaders wanted him to be the next chairman: he wrote 'I would do anything to get out of it' (4 September 1951), for he was aware of the heavy expectations on the chairman as a representative Christian figure who would be looked up to by many and the administrative burden of arranging speakers, visiting and organising the site and making arrangements for the many thousands who attended the convention in July annually. This said, he enjoyed through Keswick deep and sustaining Christian friendships with leaders like Clarence Foster, George Duncan, Hugh Orr-Ewing and Cecil Bewes to name a selection: and, although, as chairman, he did not make presentations as a main speaker, his role in presiding over the final communion services never failed to give him immense joy: the service was 'wonderful', with a sense of Christ's presence (15 July 1955), 'I loved taking it' (19 July 1957), and he felt 'near to heaven' (22 July 1960). His considerable labours were rewarded in some measure, after he retired from BCMS, by the Keswick leaders, prompted by General Wilson Haffenden, initiating tours of the Far East to India, Korea, Hong Kong and Japan, when he spoke to similar conventions as a representative of Keswick and was encouraged to take Coralie with him.

In 1955 the council (and Tim Houghton with it as chairman) faced criticism from an unexpected quarter. J I Packer, by then a member of the Tyndale Hall staff where Tim Houghton chaired the college council, had never attended Keswick but as a recently converted Christian when still at Oxford found the Christian Union heavily influenced by Keswick teaching on victorious living, teaching he found to be a personal disappointment to him and he addressed the issues in the *Evangelical Quarterly* of July 1955. His basic criticism of the entire Keswick approach was of an underlying Pelagianism, Pelagius being the British monk who, as distinct from St Augustine's overwhelming emphasis on divine grace in salvation, had been criticised for making more room for moral conduct ('works') as a part of the whole.

Tim Houghton as Chairman of the Keswick Convention
(1951-69)

Tim Houghton visiting East African
Christians in 1968

Packer pointed to Calvin and John Owen, who represented the Reformed tradition, restating that sanctification was all of grace, as Augustine had also done, drawing on St. Paul. For Packer, even so Reformed a theologian as Handley Moule had been drawn into Pelagian-style expressions on this subject in his *Outlines of Christian Doctrine* (*EQ*, p. 162 note 2). The result for Packer was that the Keswick message was 'depressing' for the Christian, because the Christian found himself/herself still engaged in a battle; and 'delusive', for the offer of deliverance from sin was untrue to both scripture and experience (p. 166). Keswick emphasis on self-consecration was too liable to a Pelagian understanding of sanctification by human effort.

There had been a history of such criticism of Keswick emphases by theologically informed evangelicals, dating back to J C Ryle, and in Tim Houghton's time Dr. Lloyd-Jones had expressed the place of Christian struggle and warfare over against any over-emphasis on a pietistic 'resting' in Christian discipleship. Packer's article was brave, as he was in a vulnerable position *vis à vis* the chairman of the college council: but, although Tim Houghton regretted the criticism, which he viewed, rightly or wrongly, as going beyond 'Christian courtesy' (13 August 1955), he was too big a man to take the issues personally, although Packer's biographer Alistair McGrath noted 'the review could not help but be seen as an attack on Tim himself' (*To Know and Serve God*, p. 78). He contented himself with writing a long letter to Packer from his annual beach holiday (25 August 1955). In their admirable and fair book *Transforming Keswick* (2000), Charles Price and Ian Randall try to set the record straight. They recognise that, even recently to their book Packer had continued to charge Keswick with 'spiritual goofiness' and the kind of retreat into pietism that he had personally striven hard to correct in the evangelicalism he inherited as a theologian in the 1950's. As they show, against this charge in Tim Houghton's time as chairman, there was a steady attempt to introduce solid and scholarly teaching from the Keswick platform, instanced by the presence of E F Kevan, weighty principal of London Bible College; and later by the introduction of John Stott, who gave memorable addresses on Romans to the convention of 1965, Michael Green, Alec Motyer and Dick Lucas, with a balancing commitment to non Anglican speakers like Graham Scroggie, Alan Redpath, Stephen Olford and Raymond Brown. Stott paid tribute to Tim Houghton's chairmanship, where he left speakers free to express their own understandings of the biblical material even when, as happened between Stott and Redpath in the 1965-8 period, their interpretation differed (*Transforming Keswick*, pp. 234-44). In relation to Packer's criticism, the New Testament itself contains the dual emphases of divine initiative and human responsibility in sanctification, in St. Paul's words 'work out your own salvation, for it is God who is at work within you both to will and to work his good pleasure' (Phil. 2:12 AV). Tim Houghton was content that people found God at Keswick and were called to a greater consecration by way of theologically informed and clear biblical teaching: as he said at the time of the Keswick centenary in 1975 in an interview with Cumbrian radio, the aim remained the pursuit of 'practical and scriptural holiness', a note he struck in his foreword to John Pollock's *The Keswick Story* of 1964, a fruit of his chairmanship.

In 1966 Tim Houghton had been present at a meeting of the Evangelical Alliance when Dr Martyn Lloyd-Jones made what became a famous, if controversial, appeal for all evangelicals to leave their various denominations in order to combine in one body (18 October 1966). He wrote in his autobiography: 'Martyn Lloyd-Jones in a forty minute address, appealed to Evangelicals to leave their churches and form a united Evangelical Church. This was quite uncalled for and John Stott felt compelled at the end to express his disagreement' He continued: 'for Anglicans, when there is a growing opportunity to witness uncompromisingly within the Church of England, it would have been a tragic step to come out'. He was no stranger to disputes with Lloyd-Jones. They had talked late into the night on issues of church establishment and the Crown (3 April 1962). By contrast to this call to 'come out from among them', CEEC was in the process of planning an Anglican Evangelical Congress, which became Keele '67, which has been held to have changed attitudes of the evangelical constituency towards greater involvement in the structures of the Church of England. Adrian Hastings wrote of its background as 'the reassertion of English Evangelicalism as being Anglican, in contrast with the far more non-denominational character of Evangelical institutions generally' and 'it greatly altered the Evangelical sense of direction. The first deliberate and public step towards closing the mental schism with most other Christians which Evangelicals had been somewhat smugly cultivating ever since 1910' (*A History of English Christianity*, pp. 553-4). Tim Houghton was involved in the earliest planning of this gathering of 1000 people. Early proposals were aired in the CEEC (11 June 1964; 19 February 1965) and planning sessions followed (30, 31 December 1965; 4 January 1966). He himself was commissioned to write one of the papers for the preparatory volume *Guidelines* (Falcon CPAS, 1967) edited by Jim Packer, who by then was on the staff of Latimer House, an Anglican Evangelical 'think-tank' in Oxford where much of the preparatory work for Keele was done. Tim Houghton's paper on mission put him in a strong writing team of Stott, Packer, James Atkinson, who was Professor of Biblical Studies at Sheffield, Michael Green, Alec Motyer, Philip Hughes and his friends Bill Leathem and Norman Anderson. His title was 'Total Commitment to Christ's Command' (pp.233-252). In it he drew attention to the lack of liberty prevailing in the mission fields, where China and Burma posed special problems; to the failure of the church historically to obey the call to mission; and to the proper approach to the resurgent religions of Hindu, Buddhist and Muslim over against historical and contemporary distortions; and to the stated aim of the Division of World Mission and Evangelism of the WCC ' to further the proclamation to the whole world of the Gospel of Jesus Christ, to the end that all men may believe in Him and be saved'. He added: 'every Evangelical would heartily endorse this aim' (p. 245). Experience had shown that voluntary societies were better organs of mission than whole churches for the fulfilling of the missionary mandate. He challenged all his hearers and readers with their inescapable responsibility for Christian witness. Obedience to Christ was the final motivation for mission (p. 252).

He described the final stages of the Keele Congress held over two and a half days (April 4-7, 1967) in his autobiography: John Stott, Michael Green, Philip Crowe (in the past, curate of Tim Houghton's church at Cockfosters) and Norman Anderson 'had been up half the night drafting' the Keele statement in its final form. Tim himself tried unsuccessfully to have reference to charismatic gifts deleted from it but reference, if without any agreement, remained (6 April 1967; Keele Statement, p. 22). Reflecting upon the congress after the event he, like Adrian Hastings, saw it as highly significant: '(it) certainly proved to be a milestone in Evangelical thinking' (p. 260). Tim Houghton, whose grasp of ecclesiology and its importance is evidenced in his journals, could discern that, as regards Evangelicals and their commitment to the Church of England, Keele had taken a different and definitive route from the appeal of Lloyd-Jones that they should leave mixed ecclesial bodies for the greater purity of separatism. As he had told Geoffrey Fisher, he was both a 'definite evangelical' and an 'Anglican by conviction'.

CHAPTER 9

RETIREMENT 1966 – 1993

In a recent study, Rob Warner's *Reinventing English Evangelicalism 1966-2001*, biographers are given a salutary warning. This author divides such works of biography into critical works and hagiography. With what may be scant justice, both Timothy Dudley-Smith's two volume life of John Stott and Alister McGrath's life of Jim Packer are regarded as hagiography. There can be little doubt that so established a critical writer as F W Dillistone, who wrote the life of Max Warren, Tim Houghton's friend, contemporary and fellow general secretary of a missionary society, would be classed as a hagiographer, if only because he announced at the outset of his work that Warren was the closest thing to a saint he had met: 'I have often heard warnings about the perils of hagiography. I can only say that this man came nearer to my own conception of what constitutes a saint than any other I have known' (*Into All the World*, p. 6). Plainly some critical distance from the subject is desirable and can be rightly expected: in this final chapter of general assessment some such attempt must be made.

Warner's study began with the year in which Tim Houghton retired, a year (1966) which he regarded as 'climacteric'. In his own account he had found that Fowler's Concise Oxford Dictionary defined this word as 'constituting a crisis; occurring at a period of life at which force begins to decline; critical period in life'. He made no secret of the fact that he did not want to retire aged 70. Apart from being the son of a father who had continued in harness until the age of 90, he was in many respects at the height of his influence in the Conference of British Missionary Societies (CBMS), as chairman of Keswick, chairman of the CEEC and as a representative figure in conservative evangelicalism whose contribution was sought and respected by leading figures in the ecumenical movement. A friend like Harry Sutton, general secretary of the South American Missionary Society (SAMS), urged him to delay his retirement and he himself wanted to continue at least until the age of 73 when his chairmanship in CBMS came to an end. He found however that in the prevailing climate there was an expectation at BCMS headquarters that he would go at 70: and after considerable heart-searching and soundings with others (he laid particular weight on the advice of John Stott) he decided to retire after 21 years as general secretary. Max Warren had retired three years previously from CMS, curiously enough after the same number of years in office (1942-63): and by then his brother Frank had also retired from his parish in Leamington Spa.

Warner's study paints a picture of evangelicalism prior to 1966 as a kind of undifferentiated unity, what he terms a 'calvinistic hegemony', presided over by such figures as Dr Martyn Lloyd-Jones but destined to break up into new manifestations which included the charismatic movement. Professor Brian Stanley disputed this pre-1966 picture and singled out 'A T Houghton' as one sign of pluralism and a differing voice in conservative evangelicalism: 'here was the leader of the missionary society created by the most notable 'fundamentalist' secession in British evangelical history taking a public stance against separation', that is, against the kind of call Lloyd-Jones has made to evangelicals to leave their mixed bodies. In Stanley's opinion here was a sign, in Tim Houghton's stance, that 'conservative evangelicals had emerged from the fundamentalist ghetto into the realm of ecumenical dialogue… about to enter an era of prominent and unprecedented influence' ('Post War British Evangelicalism' p. 18)

Apart from the Keele Congress of 1967, already examined here, the late 1960's faced Tim Houghton with serious issues affecting the Bristol colleges which made for a far from relaxed retirement. As chairman of both the Tyndale Hall college council and that of the women's college at Dalton House he was deeply involved in developments. In February 1968 the de Bunsen Report on Theological Colleges pointed to fresh approaches and to larger colleges: college mergers became a pressing issue between 1968-

71. He had noted in his journal that the Tyndale Council had little hope of cooperation with Clifton (10 January 1968). Feelers were put out to see whether Tyndale and Dalton House might join the re-constituted London College of Divinity in its new setting in Nottingham (now, St John's, Nottingham) (14 February 1968). A further impetus was supplied by the archbishops' report suggesting that Tyndale and Clifton should merge, as also Wycliffe and Ridley (21 February 1968). While he reported that the councils of Tyndale and Clifton were open to meetings, a document produced by the staffs of the colleges 'made very sad reading', which caused both councils to conclude that there were 'insuperable obstacles' against the two staffs meeting (3 July 1968). By October, however, a joint college under a commonly chosen principal was acceptable as a proposal and the man chosen was Michael Baughen, then incumbent of Holy Trinity, Platt, Manchester and later at All Souls, Langham Place and Bishop of Chester. After his invitation (25 October 1968) he expressed the wish to have Julian Charley, then at All Souls, as his Director of Studies, though the Clifton negotiators insisted that Jimmy O'Byrne must be vice-principal in the uniting college (7 November 1968). All this however unravelled. O'Byrne resigned in December and members of the Clifton staff refused to meet with Michael Baughen (24 January 1969). There was a further meeting of six and a half hours; further disputes about the basis of faith to be adopted by the future college, though agreement to the suggestion that 'Trinity College' should be its name (13 February 1969). Agreement could not be reached and this led to the eventual withdrawal of both Michael Baughen and Julian Charley in what Tim Houghton described as a 'very tragic' outcome (16 May 1969).

This long running saga has been well described by Alister McGrath in his life of Jim Packer (*To Know and Serve God*, pp. 138-179). For Tim Houghton the next development was the resignation of the principal of Tyndale Hall, Stafford Wright, in 1969, which led to the appointment of Jim Packer at a time when, in McGrath's words, student numbers were 'dangerously low' (p.151); with only 28 students in residence and a probable financial loss of £7000 for the year predicted. Packer assembled a strong team to staff the college, with Alec Motyer as vice-principal (who had previously resigned from Clifton staff), Anthony Thiselton, Colin Brown and John Tiller. In 1970 the colleges were confronted with the Runcie Report, which again pressed for mergers, with further advice provided by an evangelical working party chaired by John Stott, which recommended a merger of Clifton, Tyndale and Dalton House in Bristol as the best of the variety of options which it presented. This was in contrast to the Runcie recommendations, which had eliminated Bristol as a centre for training altogether, with Clifton going to Wycliffe in Oxford and Tyndale to Nottingham. Between November 1970 and January 1972 there were a series of increasingly urgent meetings, with various options canvassed and the bishops demanding the closure of Tyndale Hall (5 February 1971) from the beginning of the academic year in October 1971. The Bishop of Bristol, Oliver Tompkins, offered his services as chairman of a joint meeting of the councils of the three colleges, conditional on the resignations of all staff and governors towards the new provisions. Tim Houghton pressed for and achieved a working party from the councils on the new 'Trinity College' (4 March 1971) and the Bishop of Bristol chaired meetings of the three councils in April and May (27 April, 21 May 1971). Despite last minute battles in regard to Packer's position and that of others (McGrath, p. 176) Tim Houghton wrote that 'the bishop (of Bristol) is not going to stand any more nonsense' (17 September 1971) and at a meeting held in conjunction with the consecration of Maurice Wood as Bishop of Norwich on September 29 it was agreed that Packer would become associate principal with Alec Motyer and Joyce Baldwin in a triumvirate. The college aimed to have a total of 80 students (29 September 1972).

Retirement also meant foreign travel. As noted above, the Keswick leadership facilitated a tour of the Far East for both Tim and Coralie in 1967. This included visits to India (where he met Indira Gandhi (8 January 1967)) and a visit to Amy Carmichael's home at Dohnavur (20 January) and to such centres as Bangkok, Hong Kong, Japan and Seoul, where some 6-7000 people attended in three services. On this tour he calculated that he spoke around 100 times. He organised the first of a number of Holy Land tours in July 1967, which took a great deal of careful administration for the tour operators in the gathering of personnel and the oversight of visits to the Biblical sites, a form of activity greatly enjoyed but increasingly demanding. For BCMS he undertook a tour of their work in East Africa in 1968, where once again he was able to locate the Kensington Chapel organ of his boyhood still in use (27 August 1968). At home he continued to act as chairman of the Keswick Convention until 1969, remaining on the Council till 1980, a stint of 35 years, during which the illness of John Caiger as chairman led to his recall: he finally retired from the Keswick Council but became, with Cecil Bewes his friend and contemporary, a trustee (12

May 1981). Annual visits to Bude on holiday gave much enjoyment, often involving visits to the CSSM beach mission, as well as surfing, bathing and much holiday reading. He remained as president of the Missionary School of Medicine until 1977 and became a vice-president of BCMS (8April 1968), which entitled him to attend BCMS meetings on a regular basis and to make some strategic interventions over policy during Alan Neech's term of office, a successor with whom he retained a strong friendship and good working relationship, highly satisfied that Neech succeeded him as a chairman of Keswick and to his position on the Conference of British Missionary Societies (CBMS), of which he himself became vice-president. Although he handed over the chairmanship of the Church of England Evangelical Council (CEEC) to John Stott in 1966, he continued as a member of the council for some years and of the Evangelical Fellowship in the Anglican Communion (EFAC) until 1980, while remaining as vice-chairman of the EFAC Bursary Fund, which involved much paper work on the various overseas candidates: in the wider church, he also served on the Overseas Bishoprics' Fund. This, with his full range of speaking engagements at home, which included Christmas Day Holy Communion at 8am until 1984 at Christ Church, Barnet, when he was 88, comprised a full and active retirement, interspersed with many visits to his children and their families and his twenty-four grandchildren.

Some overall assessment of this many-sided life, and his theological and ecclesiastical position must be attempted. He would have wanted to stress that fundamental to all was his long and happy marriage to Coralie. They celebrated their Golden Wedding on 1 July 1974 and ten years later received congratulations from Buckingham Palace and Billy Graham on their Diamond Wedding, in telegrams which gave enormous pleasure. Tim Houghton was a man of prayer, to which his daily journals testify, both reflective before worship or preaching and intercessory, when confronted with the trials of his family and friends, including the fierce trials associated with the tragic loss of four grandchildren. As has been shown, he was a convinced Anglican: he could be disturbed when, for example, an Anglican church failed to observe Advent as a season with a suitable collect and hymns for the season. He understood the importance of ecclesiology, a due doctrine of the church 'so many evangelicals lack any doctrine of the church' (12 November 1959): this could make him impatient in the context of missionary societies where this aspect was disregarded. He was aware that, despite his brother Frank's and Stanley's service for the non-denominational China Inland Mission (CIM), service he had himself considered earlier in life, he fitted well (and knew it) in a society with a clear ecclesiology like BCMS rather than among what he called 'churchless people' (14 November 1957). He did not approve of certain contemporary movements either within Anglicanism or in evangelicalism. He never approved of the charismatic movement and took steps on a number of occasions to see that Keswick did not invite on to the platform those who spoke in tongues or advocated the practice, an extreme example being that of Michael Green who had proved supportive of the movement in his *I believe in the Holy Spirit* in the 1970's: he resisted attempts to invite him back to Keswick after this and referred to him as 'another broken reed' (15 August 1975), writing 'I scotched the idea of inviting Michael Green in view of his book' (29 October 1976); and he was dismayed by the Keswick Council inviting Don Bridge, who both spoke in tongues and advocated the practice (7 November 1984). Contemporary experiments like the use of dance in worship and drama (19 March 1978) he disliked and he protested when BCMS used the talented drama group, Riding Lights, in their presentation (27 June 1978; 22 September 1979).

He resolutely opposed the ordination of women (25 April 1980). At New Delhi in 1961, when the issue was raised, he confided in his diary that the day had been saved by the various Orthodox representatives (4 December 1961), who opposed it so trenchantly that his own intervention was unnecessary. He took grave exception to an article in the Church of England Newspaper written by Joyce Baldwin and Myrtle Langley, which revealed their sympathy for the Movement for the Ordination of Women (MOW) (25 April 1980). While appreciating a presentation by Rosemary Nixon of the Cranmer Hall staff on the ministry of women ('I agreed with a lot') he remained then and later unconvinced 'about the rightness of women's ordination' (7 March 1983): when the General Synod approved it in principle in 1984, he drew comfort from the fact that it would not come about until 1990 when 'I may not be around', plainly a relief to him (15 November 1984). He engaged in an exchange of views on the subject with George Carey, who accused him of being 'unscriptural' in the CEN, an unexpected charge, to which he responded, only to find that his response to the future Archbishop of Canterbury was not printed, which caused him to 'write a snorter' to the editor (22 December 1984).

He and Coralie were firm royalists. Great was the excitement when, in response to a letter from Coralie, special arrangements were made for them both to celebrate one of their wedding anniversaries by penetrating the railings of Buckingham Palace to see the Queen at close quarters, made possible by the good offices of Lady Susan Hussey, a lady-in-waiting on 1 July 1977. In politics, Tim Houghton was a committed Conservative, whose victories either in an election or in the House of Commons were greeted with 'joy' (18-19 June 1970) and 'utter joy' (28 March 1979): but he was well able to appreciate a fine speech by Michael Foot at the time of the Falklands invasion (3 April 1982) or telling appearances on television by Denis Healey or Neil Kinnock, a sign of a true democrat. His sympathies were strongly pro-Israeli over Arab-Jewish issues (17 March 1973, 4 August 1979): and, although firmly opposed to *apartheid*, he was sympathetic to white Rhodesia in its turmoils (22 August 1979).

Culturally, he found classical music enriching. A performance of Tchaikovsky could be 'absolutely lovely' (5 May 1983) and he had a collection of fine pieces on record to which he added gladly when presents permitted. Annual performances at the Albert Hall, whether of the 'Messiah' (which he loved) or at the Carol Concerts conducted in earlier years by Sir Malcolm Sargent were a fixed point in the calendar and his love of Gilbert and Sullivan operetta, dating from Army days, remained. The stage, however, remained a source of something approaching prohibition. His great friend, Bill Leathem, invited him to a performance of Hamlet and he would no more attend that than the actors' service, arranged at Cromer by Charles Searle-Barnes during his son-in-law's curacy there: it was preferable to go to the local Baptist church than to such a thing. Aware of it or not, he was an example of the weakening of such evangelical taboos by the advent of television, thoroughly enjoying shows like Dad's Army and Yes, Minister, products of highly polished professional actors. He was strongly teetotal and it is difficult to imagine his reaction to the contemporary Church of England Newspaper, carrying weekly assessments of wine to drink. An earlier generation of evangelicals had looked askance at the reading of novels but he was well able to enjoy E M Forsters's *A Passage to India* (11 August 1972), Tolstoy's *War and Peace* (27 August 1973), works of Thomas Hardy (9 September 1980) and Jane Austen's *Mansfield Park*. He was indeed a prodigious reader, regularly borrowing 500 page books from the local library, whether political memoirs (Churchill, Macmillan), military volumes (Alanbrooke, Slim, Montgomery) or big works on Alexander the Great matched by Gibbon's *Decline and Fall*, (19 August 1972). If, as Francis Bacon wrote, 'reading maketh a full man', we can be sure that Tim Houghton was never empty.

On the domestic front, he was a dog lover, from the days of 'Tiger' in Burma, to the much loved 'Flopsy' in London days. No account of his London life would be complete without reference to the Houghton's relationship with Alice Disson, known as Gerty, whom Coralie met and engaged as a cleaner in October 1949. They supported her through an abusive marriage relationship over many years, finally helping her with her divorce, Tim Houghton led her to Christ in her need and they took her and sometimes her daughter on their family holidays. It was a friendship amply reciprocated but their support in frequent crises was exemplary. Their many years in Ealing were followed by six years in Cockfosters and then to final retirement at 2, Queen Elizabeth Court, Barnet in March 1967, involving a transfer of church to Christ Church Barnet. Finally they moved to 14, Alston Court ten years later (2 June 1977).

The study *Reinventing English Evangelicalism* with which this chapter began quoted from Max Warren's booklet of 1944 *What is an Evangelical?* in order to make the point of the increase of evangelical influence. Warren had written then: 'all too commonly today, an Evangelical in the Church of England is a person labouring under a sense of frustration and discouragement often so deep as to engender…an inferiority complex' (p. 7). By the time of the National Evangelical Anglican Congress (NEAC) of 1977, whether or not at the Keele Congress of 1967, this was no longer true of Anglican Evangelicals. Tim Houghton, as a well instructed Anglican, was familiar with the language of Article 6 of the 39 Articles where 'Holy Scripture containeth all things necessary to salvation' and where the teaching of the canonical books of the Old and New Testaments ('over whose authority was never any doubt in the Church') was final. Rob Warner's book showed that, in wider evangelicalism, the original basis of faith of the Evangelical Alliance of 1844 had been deliberately minimalist in its doctrinal requirements, so as to be inclusive. Since then, Warner showed how such evangelical statements of faith had tightened doctrinal requirements, and tended to become exclusive as a result, a charge he levels among others at the IVF/UCCF basis of 1981. Words like 'inerrancy' and 'infallibility' easily became touchstones of orthodoxy in relation to the Bible so that Warner can record that even the editor of *Christ and the*

Colleges, the early IVF history, Donald Coggan, was deemed dispensable by Dr Douglas Johnson when he 'balked at the infallibilist clause' (Warner p. 209, n. 3), an attempt, as Warner argued, to make doctrinal demands in excess of the standards of faith of the historic churches (p. 155, n. 23).

Tim Houghton himself was appealed to over bases of faith by the Girls' Crusader Union and it is interesting that he preferred the language of 'trustworthiness' for their scriptural basis, also used at Nottingham (NEAC) 1977, explained as (of the Bible) 'reliable in all that it genuinely affirms', so that the Church will not be misled on such vital doctrines as the person of Christ and the atonement if it follows scripture nor the Christian in the conduct of his or her daily life: 'in all matters of faith and conduct, the Bible is our supreme authority and guide, for Scripture was written for our instruction' (J. Capon, *Evangelicals Tomorrow: the National Evangelical Anglican Congress* 1977, p. 56). The theme of inclusiveness and exclusiveness runs through not only Warner's study but the evangelical tradition as a whole. Tim Houghton was well aware of evangelicals who did not hold to the IVF/UCCF basis but he was never narrow in his evangelical sympathies, as his friendship with Max Warren had shown; and his recognition in retirement of his debt as a young man to Bryan Green, his brother-in-law who had encouraged him in Christian witness, however much their views may have diverged in the 1980's, would not have altered his view of Bryan Green's *Practice of Evangelism* which was regarded as 'first class' when it appeared (20 September 1951). These wider sympathies also included Christians from very different traditions to his own among the leaders of the CBMS and WCC, contrasting with the criticism given in his hearing by the Congregationalist John Huxtable that the only people with whom conservative evangelicals would unite were other conservative evangelicals. As his booklet on New Delhi showed, he was not numbered among those who thought that his way of being a Christian was the only one: 'let us not be too proud to own that we have much to learn from others and that often we may find a common ground of fellowship in the basic doctrines of the faith of which we were not always aware' (*What of New Delhi*, pp. 57-8), which, he wanted to emphasise, did not mean 'involvement…compromising with the truth' nor 'subscribing to unscriptural error' (p. 60).

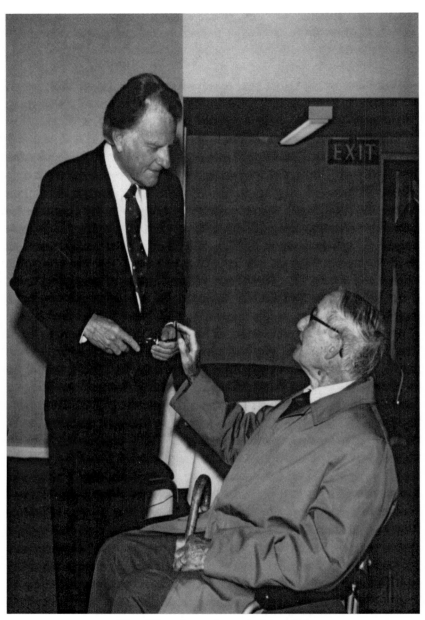

Tim Houghton (now in his 90's)
being greeted by Billy Graham at
his Earls Court crusade in 1989

Tim and Coralie enjoying their retirement in Barnet

How did others see this Christian missionary, church leader and missionary strategist? One way into this is to ask why, on so many occasions and in so many differing settings, Tim Houghton was asked to be a chairman. The good chairman needs some personal authority, to be above all a good listener able to respond to the mood and tendency of a meeting, capable of holding others to central issues without imposing his own viewpoint unduly, a clear thinker who ultimately can help others to decisions which lead into action. Tim Houghton may never have been a bishop in the technical sense but in his chairmanship he showed many of the episcopal gifts, whether in the CBMS, the Keswick Council, the CEEC or on the councils of the theological colleges like Tyndale Hall and Dalton House, not to mention on many occasions for BCMS. Canon Colin Craston, who was present frequently on BCMS occasions when he was general secretary, spoke of him as a 'kind and fair man'. John Stott, speaking at the 60th anniversary of his ordination, emphasised that his evangelical stance had always been held with 'courtesy', 'which pleased me' (19 December 1981). Many wrote in with tributes at the time of his memorial service at All Souls, Langham Place on June 26, 1993: 'Keswick never had a more godly or more gracious chairman' and from Burma and its archbishop 'the Church of Myanmar (Burma) is grateful...for years of service rendered to the Lord in our land'; while Billy Graham responded to his death: 'just heard that the Lord has called to Heaven one of his great servants on earth. He was not only a dedicated evangelical leader in Britain but a warm personal friend and supporter of mine for which I am very grateful'.

When his great friend and colleague in the Burma mission, Colonel Middleton-West, died, Tim Houghton had spoken of him using the text 'a good soldier of Jesus Christ' (12 November 1968). It was surely appropriate that this Christian leader, who as a young man had set his hopes on a field marshal's baton and as a staff officer in the 1914-18 war had shown all the administrative flair and grasp of a commander, should be described by Prebendary Dick Lucas using II Timothy 4:7 as 'fighting the good fight'. It was true of himself, as of Middleton-West, that he possessed soldierly virtues of loyalty, discipline, firmness under fire and willingness for self-sacrifice. Possibly, however, the most telling tribute of all comes from Bishop Bill Persson, who had acted as secretary when Tim Houghton was first chairman of CEEC and later made pastoral visits to him as incumbent of Christ Church, Barnet: 'he moved to live in Barnet and during my last year or so as vicar of Christ Church, Barnet, he worshipped with us. He was a considerable asset and a lovely man to visit. When one went, you not only met him, you were very much in the Lord's presence too.' No Christian could ask for a more striking memorial. The funeral address appended to this text and based on John 17 expressed eloquently the life of this twentieth century disciple, a well deserved tribute to a faithful and consecrated life of devoted Christian service.

APPENDIX I
John Stott's address at Tim Houghton's Funeral on 26 February 1993

We lay to rest today a man of God whose life spanned almost the whole of the twentieth century; and who was very close to the centre of the evangelical renaissance which has taken place during the last fifty years. To most of you or many of you he was Dad, Grandpa or Great- Grandpa. To me, because of the twenty-five years also between us, he was always 'Uncle Tim', object of much respect and affection.

As I have reflected in these last few days on his long life and his fruitful ministry, it seems to me that he had four major preoccupations which, interestingly enough, were also the four marks of the church for which our Lord Jesus prayed in John 17, which is therefore my text.

Firstly, there was his concern for the truth: in John 17 verses 6-11 Jesus prayed 'Holy Father' (I think this is the correct translation) 'keep them true to your name which you have revealed to them'. It was a prayer that God's people would always remain faithful to His (Christ's) revelation of the Father and Tim Houghton believed passionately in revelation. He was convinced that God had made himself known to us in Jesus Christ and in the total Biblical witness to Jesus Christ. So, Tim Houghton was proud all his life to be associated with the two most definite and outspoken evangelical organisations of this century, namely the Inter-

Varsity Fellowship, as it then was, of which he was a travelling secretary in the early 1940's, and BCMS whose general secretary he was for 21 years. And yet his commitment to the truth, to revealed truth, was never merely negative or defensive. He was concerned to spread the truth, to commend the truth, to make it known to others. But that I think is the first thing that we have to record about him, his concern for the truth.

Secondly, he had a concern for holiness. In John 17:15 Jesus said 'my prayer is not that you should take them out of the world but that you should protect them from the evil one'. So Tim Houghton was committed to the holiness of the people of God. He served, as you will know, as the chairman of the Keswick Council for 18 years and he sought in this way to promote what Keswick has always referred to as 'practical and scriptural holiness'. Indeed he steered the Keswick movement into the post-war world. At the same time Tim Houghton was never doctrinaire in his holiness teaching: he gave Keswick speakers full liberty to expound scripture and to teach what they believed scripture taught.

And then thirdly there was his concern for mission. Still in John 17, now verse 18, Jesus prayed 'as you sent me into the world, so I have sent them into the world'. Mission was then the third passion in Tim Houghton's life. You will remember I am sure that he toured Burma when he was serving during the First World War and came to know it on that account fairly well: and then he returned there as soon as possible after the war. He and Coralie, now married, set sail for Burma under BCMS in 1924, determined to reach the unevangelised Kachins of Northern Burma and making their headquarters at Mohnyin. Tim Houghton remained superintendent of BCMS in Burma until 1940 and he would then, as I am sure you know, have become the first bishop of Mandalay had not his ship been bombed and wrecked in 1941 and had not the Japanese overrun Burma in 1942. But Tim Houghton's inability to return to the people of Burma that he loved so well did not in any way diminish, let alone quench, his missionary zeal. As General Secretary of BCMS and then in 1960 as the chairman of the Conference of British Missionary Societies he was increasingly respected as a missionary statesman. I know that during our own annual missionary week at All Souls Church we nearly always turned to Tim Houghton to lead our missionary prayer gathering: so broad, so thorough, so rich, so balanced was his knowledge of the missionary situation in the world. Truth, holiness, mission....

Then, fourthly, his concern for unity. In verse 20 and the following verses of John 17 Jesus prayed for future generations of his disciples that 'all may be one'. We are very familiar with that prayer. To begin with Tim Houghton was concerned for the unity of evangelical people. This found expression in Keswick, whose motto of course is 'all one in Christ Jesus'. He was also chairman of the old IVF so-called 'Church of England Group', which became in 1961 the Church of England Evangelical Council, the English group member of EFAC, the Evangelical Fellowship in the Anglican Communion. But Tim Houghton's concern was not only for the unity of evangelical people. He had a concern for ecumenical unity as well. Tim Houghton had the courage as a marked evangelical leader to attend the 3rd Assembly of the World Council of Churches in New Delhi in 1961. It needed courage to do this, because in those days evangelical people had little or nothing to do with the World Council of Churches and steered clear of it as far as they were able. But not Tim Houghton: he followed his conscience and went to New Delhi. I remember quite well the meeting in the City of London which took place after his return to England in which he described his experiences, defended his decision to go and urged us also to get involved in the ecumenical movement without any doctrinal compromise.

So there are truth, holiness, mission and unity, the four marks of the church for which Jesus prayed which were also the four passions of Tim Houghton's life. I think no finer tribute could be paid to him that, whether consciously or unconsciously, he pursued throughout his life for the very things for which Christ prayed.

In conclusion, Jesus prayed for one thing more that I must not leave out in verses 24-26. 'Father' he prayed 'I want those you have given me to be with me where I am to see my glory;' and, verse 26, 'to be filled with my love'. Sometimes I know we are understandably inquisitive about the life of heaven because its precise nature continues to elude us. But for me Jesus' own description of it is enough: heaven is to be with Christ, enjoying his company, seeing his glory and being satisfied with his love. So let us rejoice and give thanks even through our tears that the prayer of Jesus has been answered in the experience of Tim Houghton. Of course, we will miss him, especially Coralie, to whom our love and sympathy are particularly directed today. Not only will she miss him but the children and the grandchildren and the great grandchildren and others who are relatives and count themselves as friends. We cannot grudge him or wish him back from that bliss into which he has entered of the glory and the love of Christ.

Appendix II
Tim Houghton's Address to the Islington Clerical Conference in 1947

ESSENTIALS IN THE INDIVIDUAL

Evangelicals have always emphasised personal religion – the need of a personal relationship with God. It is fitting, therefore, that the climax of our studies in Evangelical Essentials should concentrate on the individual.

What are the marks we should expect to find in one who calls himself an Evangelical? *Are* there essential characteristics, modes of thought, practices, which would distinguish an Evangelical from others? Or are we so keen on merging ourselves into a great homogeneous whole that we should deprecate the idea of an Evangelical being distinguishable in life and character from others of the Anglican persuasion? The suggestion of the President's invitation to this Conference is that there *are* such rock bottom essentials even in an age when the term "evangelical" appears to have a wider connotation than its original setting.

I suggest that it is in that original historical setting that we shall find most truly depicted those characteristics which have persisted in evangelical life and witness during the last two centuries, and which may be regarded as essential in the life of anyone worthy of the name of Evangelical. There have been periods in more recent history when it has been a fair criticism to say of some professing Evangelicals that they were satisfied with a heart belief in Christ and a doctrinal soundness, while less emphasis was laid on the practical outcome in the daily life. The early Evangelicals, while regarding personal religion as of the utmost importance, never divorced faith from works. "As the body without the spirit is dead, so faith without works is dead also" (James ii. 26). They were men who had their feet planted on earth while their hearts were in Heaven. It was said of William Grimshaw of Haworth that "the same Christ that he preached in the pulpit was the Christ he endeavoured to follow in his daily life" (Ryle, *Christian Leaders*, p.118).

It is in these two spheres of personal Christian experience and practical daily living, never divorced the one from the other, that we shall find the core of evangelical essentials in the individual. Combined with both is a *joie de vivre*, a joy in the Lord, and a zeal in His service, which gave to the early Evangelicals the despised name of "Enthusiasts". In polite society to be guilty of "enthusiasm" was the unpardonable sin. It was a criticism which every Evangelical should gladly bear, for no one can be called worthy of the name who is not enthusiastic in Christ's service. Lack of enthusiasm may well characterise the "Low Churchman", a term often confounded in the minds of the uninstructed with that of Evangelical, but with which the only affinity is a common freedom from ritual and ornate ceremonial in worship. Indeed, the true Evangelical may be a "High Churchman" in the Scottish sense of holding an exalted view of the Church, which is His Body.

PERSONAL RELATIONSHIP WITH GOD

You cannot study the lives of the early Evangelical leaders without realising that each one had been radically changed by a true heart conversion to God. Men who knew the plague of sin in their own hearts, the joyful experience of forgiveness and new life from above, were quite convinced of the necessity of preaching the three Rs (*R*uin by the Fall, *R*edemption by the blood of Christ, and *R*egeneration by the Holy Spirit). They had no doubt in their own minds that everyone needed a similar radical change, whether sudden and spectacular, or gradual but none-the-less real. Even though the verse is discreetly omitted to-day in *Hymns Ancient and Modern* and *Songs of Praise*, they could sing with Charles Wesley:

"He breaks the power of cancelled sin,
He sets the prisoner free:
His Blood can make the foulest clean,
His Blood availed for me."

They expressed their faith with the warm personal emphasis of St Paul in such phrases as: "I am crucified with Christ: nevertheless I live; yet not I , but Christ liveth in me: and the life which I now live in the flesh I live by faith in the Son of God, Who loved me and gave Himself for me" (Galatians ii. 20). Yet that faith was free from mysticism, and based on the *objective* fact of the Cross. It was, therefore, to be distinguished from that less robust, more mystical and sentimental type of faith brought out in the hymns of the next century, contributed by members of the Tractarian Movement, in phrases such as "Sweet Saviour", "I worship Thee, sweet Will of God"; or those that contemplate the wounds and sufferings of Christ, rather than the salvation which He wrought.

To pursue the same thread of hymnology in a later period of the last century, the essential expression of Evangelical faith must be distinguished from the familiar and sometimes almost irreverent approach to God that characterised some of the popular Sankey hymns, however much one recognises that many of those hymns have been blessed and owned of God. The early Evangelicals were so conscious of the pit from whence they were digged and of the majesty of the Triune God Whom they worshipped that they could never approach the Throne of Grace without a reverent awe in the presence of God.

In a later period still we may distinguish the essential personal religion of the Evangelical from the Pentecostal type which tends to isolate and exalt the Person of the Holy Spirit to the detriment of the Second Person in the Trinity Whom the Holy Spirit delights to honour.

Such a faith will breed a deep personal sense of unworthiness, whose outward manifestation will be a characteristic humility. In his comments on the characters of Christian Leaders, Bishop Ryle brings out the common strain of humility which runs through all. George Whitefield, William Grimshaw, Daniel Rowlands, John Berridge, Fletcher of Madeley, are all alike in this. We know how Charles Simeon regarded humility as the most important attribute of a Christian minister, and it was certainly characteristic of himself. Perhaps it is in the life of Charles Simeon that we can most easily pick out those essential marks of Evangelical religion.

Like many other Evangelicals he realised the need of maintaining the inner glow by personal communion with God. To ensure this uninterrupted quiet time he regularly rose at 4 am., and was prepared to fine himself if he failed to keep his resolve, though the extreme penalty of throwing a guinea into the Cam did not have to be repeated. Such austerity and early rising may be rare among Evangelicals today, but I venture to suggest that a regular daily time set apart for private communion with God in prayer and Bible reading is still an essential mark of the true Evangelical, and that abandonment of such a practice soon shows itself outwardly in a life lived on a lower spiritual level.

DEVOTION TO THE WORD OF GOD

With this emphasis on the importance of maintaining close fellowship with God Himself, Simeon had a great love for the Word of God. That again is characteristic of all true Evangelicals. Everything is brought to the touchstone of God's Word, which is the final court of appeal. The Bible is the chief textbook, and its principles colour the whole of life. It is "profitable for doctrine, for reproof, for correction, for instruction in righteousness: that the man of God may be perfect, throughly furnished unto all good works" (2 Timothy iii. 16, 17).

Though no true Evangelical despises scholarship or the consensus of opinion of the Church down the ages on the interpretation of Scripture, he holds to that right of private judgement which enables him to expect God to bring a personal message to himself in the reading of God's Word. As Simeon said: "The poor man who is conversant with his Bible, needs not to go to the philosopher, and consult with him; nor need he regard the maxims current in the world. With the Scriptures as his guide, and the Holy Spirit as his instructor, he needs no casuist, but an upright heart, no director, but a mind bent upon doing the will of God." Simeon had no doubt about the divine inspiration of the Holy Scriptures: he affirmed that "God is the author of them, and that every part of them has been given by inspiration from Him."

From the study of the Scriptures and the constraining love of Christ the Evangelical must develop a love for the souls of others and a longing to bring them into touch with Christ as a living Saviour. Simeon was no stranger to this longing, both in and out of the pulpit. On the subject of preaching he gave as a motto the couplet:

"I'd preach as though I ne'er should preach again,
I'd preach as dying, unto dying men."

Is it going too far to say that the sermons of many modern Evangelicals contain no bite or vital message because they contain too much of human vapourings and too little of God's Word, and that sometimes when an Evangelical has an evangelistic gift, too much emphasis is laid on the personal appeal divorced from a solid doctrinal basis of teaching? The early Evangelicals built on a strong foundation of theology anchored to the Word of God.

The final characteristic, common to all the outstanding Evangelicals of the past, was that of holiness of life. Holiness always involves separation: separation *unto* God (set apart for His service) as well as separation *from* the world. It is true that as a result of the Keswick Convention and similar movements in the modern world, there has been a greater general emphasis on the need for holiness, and the consecration of the whole man to Christ's service; but such wholehearted consecration was equally characteristic of many of the earlier Evangelicals. They lived in a world where material values were in the ascendant, as we do even more emphatically today, but there were no half measures in their allegiance to Christ's commands. The true Evangelical has always opposed the ascendancy of the spirit of worldliness in the Church and has supremely stood for spiritual values. At the same time the early Evangelicals stood for an intensely practical Christian relationship to the world around. While not "of" it they were definitely "in" it.

THE EXAMPLE OF WILLIAM WILBERFORCE

Perhaps one of the best examples to bring out the essential marks of an Evangelical in practical daily living is that of William Wilberforce, whose life bears the hallmark of holiness, while in the midst of an environment of public life, which, it might be argued, would be inevitably detrimental to spiritual progress. There is an interesting chapter in Coupland's life of Wilberforce entitled *The Saint* (Chapter vii), which carries all the more weight because it is written by one who might be described as an observer on the touchline and not professing himself to possess the same spiritual experience. Wilberforce had expressed his faith in his book, *A Practical View of the Prevailing Religious System*, which had such a wide circulation among the aristocracy of the time. His biographer writes of it: "The most malicious cynic could not accuse the author of the 'Practical View' of failing to practise what he preached" (*The Saint*, p. 199).

The whole record of Wilberforce's public life is one which emphasises what should be regarded as an essential counterpart of Evangelical faith – sterling Christian *character*, sadly lacking in much of the Christian profession of this generation. There was a balance about his life which made it possible for him to live in society, and be a welcome guest in the houses of those who made no Christian profession, and yet to remain in separation from the things that were essentially worldly. His moral courage, which always commanded the respect of the younger Pitt, a lifelong and intimate friend, was shown not only in his witness in pagan society, but in his consistent fight for the abolition of the Slave Trade through long weary years of waiting, at great personal sacrifice, and regardless of its effect on his political career, and the loss of the friendship of some in high places.

Men could rely on his word, and know that a promise would be kept. As Coupland says: "His association with any enterprise was accepted by the public as a proof, not always of its wisdom, but always of its honesty. ... Wilberforce's name, in fact, became a by-word for scrupulous virtue" (*The Saint*, p. 201). Certainly the statement in the "Gentleman's Psalm", delightfully phrased in the Prayer Book version, would be true of him: "He that sweareth unto his neighbour, and disappointeth him not: though it were to his own hindrance" (Psalm xv. 5.). Surely this *should* be an essential mark of the Evangelical today, that a man should be absolutely reliable and trustworthy, and command the confidence of all with whom he deals?

Because of his readiness to witness for Christ in high places, Wilberforce not only made use of his opportunities, but exercised an influence that has persisted to the present day. Read the account of the way he spent his Sundays (*The Saint*, p.188): family prayers in his own household, morning and evening worship in Church, and an afternoon given up to helpful reading, and this in the midst of a busy political life which often taxed his strength to the utmost. He saw the importance of the divinely-appointed Day of Rest in the suicides and breakdowns of his own contemporaries who worked seven days a week, and his own example had an effect on the world outside. It was Wilberforce who was the means of bringing about the abolition of Parliament's assembling on Mondays, so as to avoid the necessity of Sunday travelling, and who prevented the victimisation of those who, for conscience' sake, refused to drill on Sundays in face of the threatened Napoleonic invasion. A Wilberforce, patriot as he was, might have done much to mitigate the lot of the Home Guard in the last war, if he had been alive, and would have had the moral courage to speak out. His biographer states: that "it was largely owing to these personal efforts on Wilberforce's part that a stricter observance of the Sabbath came into general vogue by the end of the eighteenth century" (*The Saint*, p. 189). Whatever the cares of the week it was said of Wilberforce that "on Sunday, at any rate, he was incorrigibly happy" (*The Saint*, p. 190).

We may smile at Wilberforce's "launchers", as he called his carefully prepared openings for speaking to his pagan friends about the things that matter most, but his gay and exuberant spirit provided him with opportunities, and his love for the souls of men was not confined to his own friends, but showed itself in his active support from the time of the foundation of such organisations as the Bible Society and Church Missionary Society, and in his generous, sacrificial giving to all good causes.

DOCTRINE AND LIFE

At the close of his book on *Christian Leaders*, Bishop Ryle asks this pertinent question – written in the nineteenth century, but even more applicable today:

"Wherein do Evangelical Churchmen fall short of their great predecessors in the 18th century? ... They fall short in *doctrine*. They are neither so full or so distinct, nor so bold, nor so uncompromising. They are afraid of strong statements. They are too ready to fence, and guard, and qualify all their teaching, as if Christ's Gospel was a little baby, and could not be trusted to walk alone. They fall short as *preachers*. They have neither the fervour, nor fire, nor thought, nor illustration, nor directness, nor holy boldness, nor grand simplicity of language which characterised the last century. Above all, they fall short in *life*. They are not men of one thing, separate from the world, unmistakeable men of God, ministers of Christ everywhere, indifferent to man's opinion. regardless who is offended if they only preach truth, always about their Father's business, as Grimshaw and Fletcher used to be. They do not make the world feel that a prophet is among them, and carry about with them their Master's presence, as Moses when he came down from the mount." (*The Saint*, p. 430).

We lack both the men and the message of the 18th century. What wonder if we do not see this century's results. Give us like men and a like message, and I have no fear that the Holy Ghost would grant us like results." (*The Saint*, p. 430)

Let us hear the conclusion of the whole matter. Is it not essential to every individual Evangelical that in the quiet of his own heart he should be able to say with Charles Simeon, as quoted by Dr Charles Smyth in the concluding paragraph of his book on *Simeon and Church Order*:

"While I am here, I am a sinner – a redeemed sinner; that is my style; and as such I would lie here to the last, at the foot of the Cross, looking unto Jesus; and go as such into the presence of my God." (*op.cit*, p. 312).

APPENDIX III
BBC Radio Cumbria's Interview with Tim Houghton in July 1982

(Our thanks to BBC Radio Cumbria for giving permission to include this interview)

Introduction by Nigel Holmes: The BBC World Service broadcast service from the Keswick Convention in its centenary year 1975 was chaired by Canon Tim Houghton. Canon Houghton's daughter now lives at Wetheral near Carlisle and, whilst he was staying there, he told me about his long life, about his association with the Keswick Convention and also about his many years in the mission field in the Far East. He began by telling me of his first journey to that part of the world during the First World War.

Tim Houghton: I was drafted into the army into the Somerset Light Infantry. I came from Bath then. First of all we were on a draft to go to France where I wanted to go as my brother was killed at the Battle of the Somme. But in the end we were sent as a draft to join a battalion of the Somerset Light Infantry in Burma. That's how I came to Burma in the first instance.

Nigel Holmes: Had you previously had any interest or knowledge of the Far East?

Tim Houghton: Oh yes. I was quite definitely going to be a missionary. All my early years I wanted to go into the Army, that was a great interest. But when I had what I believed to be was a definite call from God to go to the mission field, I started preparing for that – so I took an interest in mission work everywhere.

Nigel Holmes: Seems strange that it was either to be a soldier or a missionary.

Tim Houghton: Yes, I suppose it was. But I used to argue, when my father was very much against me going into the Army (my father being a vicar in Bath), that there were great Christian soldiers like General Gordon and why shouldn't I be a Christian soldier.

Nigel Holmes: The First World War of course forced you into that mould.

Tim Houghton: In fact it gave me the fulfilment of my ambition. I had three and a half wonderful years which I enjoyed fully.

Nigel Holmes: Was it a tough time then?

Tim Houghton: I suppose it might have been called a tough time in the ranks first of all; then on a cadet unit and a commission; back to my old regiment but another battalion; and then ending up on the staff at army headquarters, so I had a very good time really.

Nigel Holmes: So did that really satisfy you, and after that you felt that the mission field was the right place for you?

Tim Houghton: Yes quite definitely. All along I had never given up the idea. Wherever I went, particularly when I was staff officer to the Inspector of Infantry, I used to send my programmes to various missionaries I heard of in places where I went to. So I could see something of the work that was going on at the same time.

Nigel Holmes: I gather also that at that time you saw something of the Border Regiment.

Tim Houghton: Yes, they were one of the two British battalions in Burma at that time – the 4th Border Regiment and the 5th Somerset Light Infantry. I was in the Somersets and we were sent to a cadet unit in the Punjab; and there were about seven or eight men from the Border regiment, including the Regimental Sergeant Major. We got our commissions then in India and of course we then dispersed after that in various regiments.

Nigel Holmes: Was it as a result of that connection with Cumbria that after the First World War you came first to the Keswick Convention more or less almost straightaway?

Tim Houghton: It was nothing to do with that. But I have always felt a rather interesting connection with Cumbria because of that contact with the Border Regiment and took a great interest in them and their history. But it was as a student at a theological college straight after the war that I went to the Keswick Convention in 1920.

Nigel Holmes: What did you remember of that first occasion because clearly going back more than fifty years it must be very different now from what it was then?

Tim Houghton: The thing that struck me was that here were some thousands of young people, a good many with bibles under their arms, and all seeming happy with their religion; and I had lived for several years in India and Burma hardly meeting any Christians at all, at various times and in very small numbers. To see these thousands of people all listening to bible readings and so on, struck me as being a tremendous thing,

Nigel Holmes: Was it something of an upper class gathering at that time because you had a very strong contingent from the universities there?

Tim Houghton: Yes, I suppose so, more so than today. But it was a pretty good mixture from every walk of life.

Nigel Holmes: And would you hear the great preachers of the day?

Tim Houghton: Yes, people like Graham Scroggie, Bishop Taylor Smith. I heard Webb-Peploe at his last time at Keswick, I think, and he had been speaking at Keswick from the foundation in 1875.

Nigel Holmes: Did any one particular speaker make a particularly long-lasting impression on you?

Tim Houghton: Yes, a man named Russell Howden who spoke on the Holy Spirit, and that address was more help to me than anything else I think.

Nigel Holmes: And then after a short time back in the country both at theological college and at Durham University for a time, you went back out to the mission field and the Far East.

Tim Houghton: In 1924. By that time I was married and one of my sisters was a nurse, so she was sent out with us. We went to the far north of Burma, 660 miles from Rangoon at a place called Mohnyin, where we were amongst the people whom I had seen in December 1918 when I had visited Burma with my general and he inspected a military police battalion in Myitkyina, the farthest northern part of the Burma Railways where these people called the Jinghpaw lived in the hills and were being recruited by the army. It was to those people I felt that God was calling me. Today there are thousands of Christians in that area there where there were none before.

Nigel Holmes: This was very much pioneer missionary work with a pioneer society?

Tim Houghton: Yes, it definitely was. It was the only Anglican work in the north. But the American Baptist Mission had been working over the border of China and Burma amongst the same people. In fact one of their missionaries had translated the Bible, so we had a very good start to our work in pioneer territory.

Nigel Holmes: Did you find it fairly easy to establish relationship with the people there?

Tim Houghton: Our main effort was through medical work. I had taken a short medical course before I went out to Burma – and at one time I had wanted to be a doctor – and my sister of course was a trained nurse, a hospital sister. We started a dispensary which attracted people from the hills; and that is how we got openings into villages where patients had been successfully healed and treated.

Nigel Holmes: And so, gradually you built up quite a considerable Christian community.

Tim Houghton: Yes, in the end we had four hospitals in different parts of Burma; and we were working amongst people of many other races besides the particular people we had begun to work amongst.

Nigel Holmes: Did you stay out there for quite a long time?

Tim Houghton: Fifteen years; and five years after that, or five or six years, I was expecting to go back but I was held up by the last war.

Nigel Holmes: During the time you were out there I imagine there were many amusing things, strange things that happened too in that totally different culture.

Tim Houghton: Almost every day was quite exciting because we were in uncivilised jungle territory where the only way you could get about was by riding ponies we had. No made roads, no cars. There were tigers and panthers and wild elephants in that area. So we were never without some excitement either with patients brought in who had been mauled by tigers; or going out ourselves into the hills and meeting with all sorts of interesting encounters.

Nigel Holmes: Did you ever come close to tragedy and danger?

Tim Houghton: No, I don't think so…well there were times. I did a lot of prospecting on my own just with a Jingphaw attendant, riding ponies. We were looking out for new areas where no missionary work had been. So I did have some quite exciting experiences in meeting with people in areas where there had been slavery before and opium poppy, unadministered territories that the government had just taken over. They only allowed us to go in provided we would establish medical work there. We had a hospital right in a place called the Hukawng Valley in the far north.

Nigel Holmes: Were the people ever hostile?

Tim Houghton: Yes, sometimes. I remember I went out to baptise a woman in a lonely village who'd come to trust in Christ herself and lived with a brother-in-law (she was a widow) and his two half-baked sisters. He was a dimsa or sacrificing priest. When I said I would come out and baptise her in her village, the message came back that, if I did, he would finish me off. But that didn't prevent me from going and in the end, although she had to leave her village, she was baptised and witnessed faithfully in a neighbouring village where she had relatives.

Nigel Holmes: So there was hostility from the indigenous religion?

Tim Houghton: Yes, there was quite a lot of hostility which gradually grew less, I think, as time went on. Certainly the medical work was greatly appreciated. People would often say 'In a few years time we will give up sacrificing to the spirits and we will follow the Jesus way'. That happened in some cases but it was rather vain empty promises in others. But today as a result of that pioneering work there are thousands of Christians in that area.

I had a letter only last week from a man who was the first Jingphaw to be ordained into the Anglican Church in Northern Burma who is retired now. He said that there are more Christians in that area now than people who offer sacrifices to the spirits which is very encouraging.

Nigel Holmes: It must be very rewarding for you who have been involved at the beginning so to speak.

Tim Houghton: It certainly is. I feel it has been tremendously worthwhile.

Nigel Holmes: There is nothing you regret about your time out there?

Tim Houghton: None at all. All our family were brought up there and it was the best days of our lives, I think.

Nigel Holmes: Have you been back there recently?

Tim Houghton: In 1966 all missionaries were expelled by the Marxist dictatorship that took over. No missionaries have been allowed in Burma since. But it has been possible to get a visa for as much as a week. My wife and I went back. We were on a speaking tour in the Far East speaking on behalf of the Keswick Convention. We got a twenty-four hour visa to visit Rangoon. Clergy and others came 600 miles from the north to meet us.

We talked non-stop for the twenty-four hours before we had to leave. It was wonderful!

Nigel Holmes: You were also thwarted on your attempted return to that part of the world just before the war?

Tim Houghton: Yes, I came home in July 1939 expecting to go back after a few months as Assistant Bishop in the Diocese of Burma, with a view to forming a new diocese in the northern part. I was held up by the war breaking out; and finally, getting a passage to go back in 1941, I think three or four times my consecration was arranged either in London or in Rangoon or in Calcutta. When I started out, we were attacked from the air three days out of Liverpool somewhere south of Iceland and our ship set on fire and a good many casualties. We got into lifeboats and we were eventually picked up and brought into Stornoway in the Isle of Lewis and so home. I got a cable from the Bishop of Rangoon asking me not to attempt to come out again until the war was over.

Nigel Holmes: So you came closer perhaps than anybody to be a bishop but not actually to be one.

Tim Houghton: Yes, that's true.

Nigel Holmes: Then you took on a new role, an administrative role with the missionary society after that.

Tim Houghton: Yes, I was asked to become General Secretary of the society I had worked under, the Bible Churchmen's Missionary Society, which had work in various parts of the world in Asia and Africa.

Nigel Holmes: And you took charge of that work?

Tim Houghton: I took charge of that work, and so for some years during that time I frequently visited areas of our work in India and east Africa and other countries.

Nigel Holmes: And that work continues to this day?

Tim Houghton: That work continues, although it's been curtailed. There are no missionaries in Burma now, none in China as there were in Western South China, none in Ethiopia. But in East Africa mainly our work is concentrated now and in some parts of India.

Nigel Holmes: After the war you renewed your relationship with the Keswick Convention. Obviously, when you had been away, you had been unable to attend. But you became once again a regular attender and then held fairly prominent and high office.

Tim Houghton: Yes, in 1945 just after the Second World War ended, I was invited to join the Council of the Keswick Convention; and I was on that council until I was appointed Chairman in 1952 and remained as chairman for twenty-one years.

Nigel Holmes: What was it that made you think of coming back and taking such a prominent part in the organisation of the convention at that time?

Tim Houghton: Well, I had always been interested in the Convention from the first time I went as a student in 1920, and was in touch with a number of people who were involved in the Convention. When I was asked to join the Council, I felt this was a responsibility I ought to take and to my great surprise I was appointed Chairman in 1952.

In those days there was no suggestion of retirement from the position and I went on and on, elected three years at a time, until I said it was about time someone else was appointed. So we drew up some rules so that no one can be chairman for more than six years at the outside.

Nigel Holmes: And you were chairman for how long?

Tim Houghton: Twenty-one years.

Nigel Holmes: So that will stand as an all-time record?

Tim Houghton: Yes, it was. Evan Hopkins of course was the one who was the longest chairman before that. I think he was chairman for sixteen years, not my twenty-one.

Nigel Holmes: What are the highlights that come back to your mind from that period of twenty-one years, coming up to Keswick each year and of course being involved in the organisation apart from that actual week of Keswick?

Tim Houghton: Well, I think one thing, without any advertisement every year Keswick was doubled in its population by those attending the convention – usually five thousand residents and two or three thousand coming in on day visits. It was the crowd of people and their background that interested me so much, particularly in relation to those who came from overseas. Every year we had about a thousand missionaries on furlough and nationals from other countries who came to the Keswick Convention.

They all came for the one purpose of meeting with God. The founder of the Keswick Convention Canon Harford-Battersby used to say that it was for the promotion of personal, practical and scriptural holiness; and it has remained true to the slogan from the beginning.

Nigel Holmes: Did you meet the founder yourself?

Tim Houghton: Oh no, he died in the eighties of the last century. But I did meet Prebendary Webb-Peploe who spoke at the first Convention in 1875 and spoke at his last Convention in 1920.

Nigel Holmes: Did you speak at the Convention yourself?

Tim Houghton: I didn't as chairman, but I spoke on several occasions before I became chairman.

Nigel Holmes: It always strikes me as somewhat surprising that, although organised religion has declined this century, a gathering like Keswick seems to have increased in size and increased in strength over the years. It's never suffered in the way that organised religion, whatever denomination, has suffered outside.

Tim Houghton: No, that's true. It has always appealed to young people. Every year I suppose about 50% of the audience are people who have come for the first time. We always try it out on the first night to find out. About half have been before and about half are there for the first time. The half that have been there for the first time consist of a very large number of young people from all walks of life, students and, in the second week that we have now had for some years now which we call the Holiday Convention Week, when families are specially catered for and the children looked after, there are always a large number of teenage children there as well as grown-ups.

Nigel Holmes: Are they then young people who are seeking some understanding of life?

Tim Houghton: I think that by and large they come from churches that are interested in the Convention and support the Convention, though a very great many come from other churches or not from churches at all. In spite of the fact that the Convention is specially meant for strengthening the lives of people who are already Christians, every year there are some who find that they have never really become Christians and are converted as a result of the Convention.

Nigel Holmes: Is it then the thing about the Convention that it is non-sectarian?

Tim Houghton: I think that is a wonderful thing that when we get there, we hardly know to what denomination anybody belongs. We are 'All one in Christ Jesus', which is the motto of the Keswick Convention.

Nigel Holmes: Why do you think that Keswick can succeed where others seem continually to fail in bringing the churches together?

Tim Houghton: I can only feel that there are so many people who are praying for the Convention; and the Council all along has been determined to keep to the old paths and to present the same message, though obviously with a modern nomenclature. But God has wonderfully protected the Convention from the changes that might have taken place if they had got away from the original theme.

The emphasis on practical holiness is so important that people are attracted to that. There is so much hypocritical religion – profession without any change of life. The fact that Keswick emphasises a practical Christian life, the daily life lived by faith in Christ and following his leadership. I think that is perhaps one of the things that attracts. The other is that here you have, despite the vain efforts of the ecumenical movement to unite people, a means by which people are united whatever their denomination maybe. They are united as Christians, they are all one in Christ Jesus.

Nigel Holmes: Did you ever face though, when you were chairman for those twenty-one years, any criticism from the churches outside who said that Keswick was Christian elitism of a kind?

Tim Houghton: Yes, again criticism that said that Keswick didn't deal with the practical problem of the day. It could easily have been a battleground for politics and all sorts of things with which people are concerned in their daily life. But the purpose of Keswick has been to enable people to keep first in seeking the kingdom of God and his righteousness; and then living out in their daily lives that which will be of practical help in the world at large.

Nigel Holmes: Does it not happen though that it is rather a letdown when the Keswick week's over? It must be terribly thrilling when you are in that large tent with so many people who are committed to one cause. It must be a great contrast surely to go back home and be relatively isolated.

Tim Houghton: Yes, that is what is emphasised in the closing day or so of the Convention that people are going down from this happy spiritual atmosphere to the environment in which they lived before. It may be an environment even in the home of opposition and persecution, and they have got to face that knowing that it is only in the strength of Christ that they can live the Christian life.

Nigel Holmes: Is Keswick itself as a town in the Lake District an ideal location?

Tim Houghton: Undoubtedly. It was providential that it was Canon Harford-Battersby who was vicar of St John's Church, Keswick that the Convention was founded there. The fact that it is in the Lake District with the lake and hills all around. A perfect setting for people to go out from the tent and sit on the mountainside and meditate the things they have heard. It's quite an ideal physical setting.

Nigel Holmes: You of course have lived the Christian life now for a great many years. Have there ever been any occasions where you have had doubts about the rightness of your life or the work you should be doing?

Tim Houghton: I don't think I have had doubts as such, except in the fact that I've been a failure as every Christian must feel that he has been a failure. It has only made me feel how wonderful is the grace of God in putting up with such poor material.

No, I've not had doubts. But I was brought up in a Christian home where my other seven brothers and sisters were brought up with me. Our parents wanted us not so much to have a success in life, as to be successful as Christians. That proved to be true in every case. Five of our family went to the mission field, one of my brothers became Bishop in West China, then Director of the China Inland Mission. It was that ideal that was set before us that stood us in good stead. I never had doubts about the fact of God's leading from the time when a hand was placed on my shoulders at a missionary meeting at the age of fourteen and I was asked 'Are you going to be a missionary?' Somehow, although it was the last thing I wanted, I knew God was speaking to me and I said 'Yes, I hope so'. And that certainty of God's leading never left me all through.

APPENDIX IV
Canon Tim Houghton 11April 1896 – 20 February 1993: Interests and Responsibilities

Superintendent of the BCMS Mission in Burma	1924-40
Travelling Secretary of the IVF	1941-44
General Secretary of the BCMS	1945-66
Chairman of the Keswick Convention Council	1951-69
President of the Missionary School of Medicine	1948-77
President of the Mount Hermon Training College	1960-71
Hon. Canon of the diocese of Morogoro, Tanzania	1965-1993
Chairman of the Asia Committee of CBMS	1966-69
Chairman of the Church of England Evangelical Council	1960-66
Delegate to the Third Assembly of the World Council of Churches at New Delhi	1961

Vice President of the Evangelical Alliance, BCMS, Crosslinks, the Lord's Day Observance Society, the Evangelical Fellowship in the Anglican Communion, the Evangelical Missionary Alliance, the Girl Crusaders' Union.

INDEX

D

Dalton House, 71, 76, 90-2, 100
Dawes, Peter (Bp), 77
Dense Jungle Green, 36, 41, 48-50, 54
Disson, A (Gerty), 96
Duffield, Gervase, 80
Duncan, George, 72, 74, 83
Durham Inter-Collegiate Christian Union (DICCU), 30, 66
Dyer, R (Gen), 20

E

Evangelical Alliance, 71, 87, 96, 125
Evangelical Fellowship in the Anglican Communion (EFAC), 71-2, 74, 93, 104

F

Fisher, Geoffrey (Abp), 67-9, 88
Foster, Clarence, 26, 72, 83
Fraser, J O, 32
Fyffe, R S (Bp), 32, 34, 38, 43, 51

G

Gardner, Dorothy, 14, 17, 21, 25, 27
Garrad, W R, 51
Gilbert and Sullivan, 14, 16, 95
Gladstone, S H, 53
Goodall, Norman, 77-8
Gore, Charles (Bp), 30-1
Gough, Basil, 77
Gough, Hugh (Abp), 20, 72, 74
Graham, Billy, 74, 93, 98, 100
Green, Bryan, 25, 27, 33, 46, 73, 97
Green, Hubert, 26, 47, 54
Green, Michael, 80, 86, 88, 94
Greenup, A W, 24
Grubb, Sir Kenneth, 73

H

Hacking, Harold, 48-9, 70-1
Harford-Battersby, T D, 82, 121, 123
Hayward, Edward, 52
Henson, Hensley (Bp), 30
Hickinbotham, J P, 73
Houghton, Agnes, 2, 4-5, 7, 19, 23
Houghton, Beryl, 52, 56, 60, 75
Houghton, Eileen, 2, 7, 33, 36-9, 44, 50
Houghton, Elizabeth (Betty), 45, 52, 56, 60-1, 65, 75
Houghton, Frank (Bp), 2-4, 7-8, 11, 14, 16, 23-4, 26-7, 33, 39, 46, 52, 75, 90, 93, 124
Houghton, Freda, 2, 4, 16, 23, 52
Houghton, Herbert, 2-3, 5-6, 10-1, 52
Houghton, Lydia (Biddy) (Dr), 2-3, 16, 23, 59, 76
Houghton, Michael, 52, 56, 60, 75
Houghton, Monica, 52, 56, 58, 75
Houghton, Pat, 37, 39-40, 45, 52, 56, 59-60, 75
Houghton, Rachel, 52, 56, 61, 65, 75
Houghton, Stanley, 3, 16, 23, 33, 39, 75, 93
Houghton, Thomas, 1-8, 33, 60, 75
Hughes, Philip (Dr), 88
Hukawng Valley, 35, 39, 44, 46, 48

I

India, 12-3, 16, 19, 92, 94
Inter-Varsity Fellowship (IVF), 25, 60, 63-8, 71-2, 78-9, 96-7, 104, 125
Islington Clerical Conference, 72, 79, 106-112

J

Jevons, F B (Prof), 30
Jinghpaws, 34, 36-8, 40-2, 49, 116-8
Johnson, Douglas (Dr), 63, 66, 78, 97
Jones, E Stanley, 20-1
Jones, Sutton, 14, 17

Prayer Book Controversy (1927-8), 38, 41, 43

Pytches, Peter, 75

R

Ramabai, Pandita, 19
Ramsey, Michael (Abp), 76
Ransom, C W, 77
Redpath, Alan, 74, 86
Rees, Tom, 74
Ruanda, 26, 68-9
Russell, S F (Dr), 35, 46, 48, 50, 55, 70
Ryan, Dorothy, 75
Ryle, J C (Bp), 78, 86, 107-8, 112

S

Saunders, E G H (Teddy), 76, 80
Savage, G (Bp), 72
Scott, George, 23
Scroggie, Graham (Dr), 26, 86, 115
Seddon, J E, 70
Set Paw, U, 50
Shans, 37-44, 50
Sharpe, Adelaide, 44, 50
Sheppard, David (Bp), 74
Simmons, Peter (Dr), 75
Singh, Sadhu Sundar, 20
Skinner, John, 79
Slim, Sir William (Field Marshal), 12, 21-2, 95
Smith, Sir Arthur (Gen), 74
Society for the Propagation of the Gospel (SPG), 32, 38, 51-2
Somerset Light Infantry (SLI), 3, 9, 14, 16-7, 113-4
Spurgeon, Charles, 12
St John's College, Durham, 24, 66
St John's Hall, Highbury (London College of Divinity), 8, 23-4, 32, 73, 76, 91
St John's, Nottingham, 91
Stanley-Smith, Algy, 26, 67, 69
Stanway, Alfred (Bp), 81
Stibbs, A M, 72, 76

Stileman, M F (May), 36, 39, 44
Stott, John (Dr), 70, 72-3, 79, 86-91, 93, 100, 102-5
Stuart, E C (Bp), 67-9
Student Christian Movement (SCM), 30, 63-4
Sundkler, Bengt, 78
Sutton, Harry, 81, 90
Sykes, Dodgson, 24, 76

T

Tailum Jan, 41-2, 44, 50
Taylor, J Hudson, 19
Taylor, J R (Bp), 73
Temple, William (Abp), 68
Thibaw, King, 17
Thiselton, A C (Prof), 91
Thompson, Peter (Dr), 75
Tiller, John, 91
Tubbs, N H (Bp), 43, 51, 71
Tyndale Hall, 47, 71, 75-6, 83, 90-2, 100

U

University College, Durham, 25, 29, 32

V

Venn, Henry, 2
Victoria College, 3, 12-3
Virgil, 3
Visser t'Hooft, W, 77-8

W

Wallis, C S, 25, 66
Walton, W C (Gen), 18-9, 21, 25
Warren, Jack, 27
Warren, Max, 27, 29, 72-4, 77-8, 89-90, 96-7
Watson, David, 79
Webb-Peploe, H W, 11, 26, 82, 115, 121
Weir, Sir John, 71

Lightning Source UK Ltd.
Milton Keynes UK
172096UK00002B/2/P